36
SMALL BUSINESS MISTAKES-
And how to avoid them

By the same author:

How to Pyramid Small Business Ventures Into a Personal Fortune.
West Nyack, N.Y. Parker Publishing Company, Inc. 1977

36

SMALL BUSINESS MISTAKES-
And how to avoid them

Mark Stevens

PRENTICE HALL
Englewood Cliffs, New Jersey 07632

Library of Congress Cataloging-in-Publication Data

Stevens, Mark.
 36 small business mistakes and how to avoid
them.
 Includes index.
 ISBN 0-13-918920-3
 1. Business. 2. Small business. I. Title.
HF5351.S82 1978   78-9800
658'.022   CIP

Printed in the United States of America

20 19 18 17 16

ISBN 0-13-918920-3

ATTENTION: CORPORATIONS AND SCHOOLS

 PRENTICE HALL
Career & Personal Development
Englewood Cliffs, NJ 07632
A Simon & Schuster Company

On the World Wide Web at http://www.phdirect.com

Prentice-Hall International (UK) Limited, *London*
Prentice-Hall of Australia Pty. Limited, *Sydney*
Prentice-Hall Canada Inc., *Toronto*
Prentice-Hall Hispanoamericana, S.A., *Mexico*
Prentice-Hall of India Private Limited, *New Delhi*
Prentice-Hall of Japan, Inc., *Tokyo*
Simon & Schuster Asia Pte. Ltd., *Singapore*
Editora Prentice-Hall do Brasil, Ltda., *Rio de Janeiro*

TO MOM AND DAD—WHOSE LOVE IS ALWAYS WITH ME

HOW THIS BOOK WILL HELP YOU

Small business owners, beware; the common mistake is still your greatest enemy. Of all the obstacles to financial success, the simple blunder is still the most devastating. That is why it is crucial to learn the pitfalls and prepare for them in advance.

This book is designed to do just that:

> to serve as your guide through the myriad of dangers that threaten novice and seasoned entrepreneurs alike. The secret is to learn from the mistakes of others—to avoid falling victim to the common blunders that topple millions of would-be millionaires.

This book charts the waters for you. I'll show you how to steer around the many dangers—both the obvious and the obscure—on your way to building a highly profitable enterprise in record time. By avoiding the typical setbacks, you'll move through an accelerated process of dynamic business growth.

All observations and recommendations are based on actual case histories observed by or related to me. The suggestions I make are gleaned from on-the-scene interviews I have conducted with small business owners across the U.S. Many of these people enjoy positions of wealth, power and prestige in their respective industries—and many have climbed up the ladder the hard way. Their combined wisdom—and their advice to you—represents more than a thousand years of top-flight business experience.

As the writer of the nationally-syndicated newspaper column, Small Business, I am in constant contact with all elements of the nation's small business community—from company presidents to United States Senators (Small Business Committee). As such, I am privy to comprehensive and often confidential information on why small companies fail and equally important, why they succeed. Now, this knowledge is available to you.

36 SMALL BUSINESS MISTAKES—And how to avoid them stresses practical solutions to real business problems. Solutions that can save you time and money. Rather than dwelling on the problems themselves I show you how to avoid them entirely. The writing is clear, concise and to the point—designed to speed you on your way to business success without delay.

You'll learn, for example, how to:

> *obtain once-secret information on IRS tax audits and how this information can save you thousands of dollars in a matter of minutes;
>
> *use a scientific formula to establish the most profitable prices;
>
> *avoid undercapitalization by projecting future cash requirements in advance;
>
> *eliminate advertising waste by learning the secrets of media selection;
>
> *avoid unnecessary taxes by getting in on the last of the super tax shelters.

All of this and more . . . much, much more. You'll get the facts, the formulas, and the business secrets you need to achieve the success you are searching for. I'll help you make it—as I have already done for thousands of others.

Although names, places and dollar amounts cited in this book have been changed, all examples cited are based on similar or typical cases observed by or related to the author. The techniques, strategies, and suggestions and other information cited in this book are based on the author's professional experience, but do not imply any guarantee of commercial or financial success.

—Mark Stevens—

TABLE OF CONTENTS

36
SMALL BUSINESS MISTAKES-
And how to avoid them

THE RUSH TO INCORPORATE:
How to find low cost alternatives

For the millions of hopefuls annually entering the ranks of the self-employed, three questions dominate most of the early planning: How do I get started? How do I form a company? Should I form a partnership, proprietorship or corporation?

Confused by the comparative benefits and drawbacks of each, all too many business owners simply avoid the issue by blindly choosing the corporate form. Why? Call it myth, error or popular misconception, the general consensus holds that the corporate form is always superior. The facts, however, do not bear this out: forming a corporation is not always the wisest choice.

The mad rush to incorporate may, in fact, adversely affect the company's future growth. Worse yet, the wrong choice of business form may cut seriously into the owner-manager's financial rewards. Not to say that incorporation is wrong or ineffective. Not in the least. It is simply crucial for entrepreneurs to examine all the alternatives before making a final choice. Although incorporation may be the ideal approach for Company A, it may offer Company B nothing more than unnecessary attorney fees and excess paperwork.

You may avoid the mistake of choosing the wrong business form by reviewing the following major types of organization:

Sole Proprietorship: Here, the emphasis is on the individual, pure and simple. For those to whom the greatest possible degree of business freedom is the overriding goal, sole proprietorship may be the ideal setup.

The sole proprietorship is the simplest type of business to start up, requires only one person to form and operate and is mostly free from governmental red tape in the organization process. All that is generally required is registration with a state or local supervisory body (check specific state requirements for details).

In sole proprietorships, business income is taxed as personal income. This can be a major benefit or drawback depending on the company's earnings and your own financial status. It is therefore wise to check with an accountant before making the final decision.

The most serious drawback of the proprietorship form is the matter of liability. In a sole proprietorship, the owner is personally liable for all claims against the business. This liability may extend to personal property and that can mean big trouble if the business falls deeply in debt.

General Partnership: In many ways, the general partnership is similar to the proprietorship form except that the partnership involves pooling the talent and experience of two or more people. Partnerships are also relatively simple to form, require only simple registration and call for income to be taxed as personal income of the partners.

Although a partnership contract is not always necessary, one is recommended. The contract should clearly distinguish each partner's rights and responsibilities in the operation of the firm. This precaution decreases the likelihood of longstanding legal disputes.

A major drawback to partnerships is that the death or withdrawal of one partner or the addition of a new partner legally terminates the partnership. Although the business may continue to function, a new contract must be drawn up every time the partnership team changes. This can prove to be a costly and time-consuming affair if the partnership is at all fluid. In addition, liabilities of the partnership do extend to the personal assets of the general partners.

The key benefit of the partnership form is the union of two or more individuals in a business venture. One may be adept at financial matters or have investment capital for the firm; others may have marketing or technical abilities. Together the individuals stand a greater chance of achieving success than if each formed sole proprietorships and tried to go it alone.

Limited Partnerships: This option offers some of the benefits of both partnerships and corporations. Here, investors in the business can become partners in it without assuming unlimited liability. The advantage of this form is that you may use it to attract investors willing to put up money but unwilling to risk personal liability.

Limited partnerships come under closer scrutiny than general partnerships. In addition, there must be at least one general partner in the firm.

Corporations: For some businesses, the corporate form is, indeed, the ideal entity. That is because corporations offer several major benefits:

*Shares of stock in the firm may be sold to selected investors or to the public. Shareholders are generally not liable for claims against the company beyond the amount invested. This can prove to be an excellent mechanism for raising capital.

*The corporation has an identity of its own. It may continue to function regardless of the death or departure of its management.

*In most cases, creditors have claims only against the assets of the corporation—officers are rarely held personally liable.

If business continuity and limited liability are not key factors, however, the corporate form can be highly inefficient for small firms. The reasons are many:

1. Corporations involve more red tape than any other type of business organization. Application must be made to state officials, charters must be granted, stock sales are regulated and lawyers must usually be hired for all of these procedures.

2. Setting up a corporation can be expensive for small operations.

Legal work and related fees can exceed $1,000 and annual franchise taxes must be paid.

3. Corporations are taxed at different rates than individuals. For many small business owners, paying corporate rather than personal taxes (available through the partnership and proprietorship forms) can mean unnecessarily heavy payments to Uncle Sam. It can mean money down the drain for no reason at all except "the mad rush to incorporate."

"I learned by doing it the hard way, but at least I learned," says Atlanta night club owner Clayton A. "After years of messing around with stock certificates, franchise taxes, paper work and lawyers, I gave up the corporate form and changed to a sole proprietorship. Now I run a business with a lot fewer headaches than I had before."

The moral is clear: Make a chart listing the pros and cons of each type of business organization. Check off the advantages and drawbacks applicable to you. Stand back and compare the results. You'll likely have the decision spelled out before you. (If still undecided, explore the issue further with your lawyer and accountant.)

CHOOSING THE WRONG PARTNER:
How to make a practical choice

A rule of thumb: Good friends make poor business partners. Like oil and water, business and social relationships simply do not mix.

The problem is one of emotions. Friendships are based on emotional ties—on sensitive handling of personal needs and feelings. The idea is to shield, protect and support friends in the trials and tribulations of their daily lives.

Although admirable in a social context, this protective instinct can have adverse effects on business operations. To be successful, business owners require accurate, straightforward information at all times. As one of our nation's leading industrialists has often stated, the top executive must insist on a policy of "no surprises." Tough, negative and even devastating information must come to the surface immediately. That's the only way to deal with a problem before it mushrooms out of control.

By attempting to shield a partner from this kind of bad news, the friend is actually doing the business a severe disservice. And that is the very reason for avoiding friendship or partnership relationships. Partners simply can not be relied on to serve up clear and objective business opinions. The preexisting emotional binds confuse and distort what must be a simple and responsive relationship.

For a partnership to be effective, both parties must pledge their basic allegiance to the company, rather than to each other. This is for the good of the business. It is far more important for the partners to worry about the performance of the company than to worry about each other while the company goes down the drain.

So while the tendency to choose a friend for a business partner is understandable, it should be avoided if at all possible. The best partnerships are based on pure business, usually with each individual bringing a certain strength to the operation of the firm.

When Doug R., an aerospace engineer from Seattle, Washington invented plans for a jet landing system, he was smart enough to shun the suggestion of his best friend and fellow engineer that they join forces in opening a company to build and market the landing system. Instead, Doug placed an ad in the Wall Street Journal and found a partner with a commodity the new company would need most: cash.

The balance was ideal. Doug's partner put up $98,000 in capital and supervised the firm's finances while Doug continued doing what he did best—inventing sophisticated equipment. Thanks to this excellent management mix, the company—Modern Flight Systems, Inc.—made it through the tough development stages and landed a million dollar plus contract with the navy. The firm was on its way.

The following checklist can be used to help select an ideal business partner or a top management aide:

1. Seek an individual capable of balancing your strengths. If you are strong in sales or marketing, pick an experienced financial or technical person. Small companies need well-rounded management.

2. Be certain the individual has had experience working with others. In most cases, a loner is a loner is a loner. Cooperation is crucial to a partnership: make sure you'll get it from the start.

3. Inquire about the person's past business experience. A prospect with a poor track record in the past is not likely to exactly provide your firm with the Midas touch.

4. Best bet is to go with an experienced entrepreneur—one who

has had experience owning and operating a private business. Inexperienced and incompetent management, after all, accounts for half of all small business failures.

5. Ascertain that the prospective partner will be equally committed to the company's success. Nothing causes more bad blood in partnerships than the feeling—right or wrong—that one partner is carrying most of the load. In most cases, demanding that your partner contribute some capital to the business will help to encourage commitment. Virtually everyone works harder when his own money is at stake.

6. Check the individual's references from schools, banks and former businesses. The last thing you want to do is wind up with a dishonest partner.

And remember—perhaps most important—limit your friends to card games and the golf course There's no room for good buddies in a business organization

SETTLING AT A DEAD-END ADDRESS:
How to find a money-making location

If you think you are fully aware of the importance of a choice business location—think again. Selecting the right business location is so important it's almost impossible to over-emphasize the point.

That's because making the wrong choice can be like running full steam ahead into a solid brick wall. For no matter how well your company is organized—no matter how finely tuned it is for financial success—simply settling at a dead-end address can throw the entire venture off course . . . permanently.

What do we mean by a dead-end address? Generally speaking, this means launching the business at a specific location which does not match the company's marketing thrust. It means settling, for one reason or another, at a site which is not conducive to generating the required sales.

This happens—and it does so frequently—when the owner-manager opts to "save money" by leasing or purchasing a place of business at a second-rate location. Or, due to ignorance or inexperience, the entrepreneur willing to spend any amount for the right spot simply makes a poor choice. Both are common mistakes you can avoid.

First, let's deal with this notion that getting in on a low rent or an inexpensive purchase price is automatically a bargain.

Nothing could be further from the truth! If there is ever a case of being penny wise and pound foolish, this is it. Investing 20, 30 or even 50 percent more to secure the best business location is just the opposite of waste: it represents productive use of business funds. It is a wise business decision.

Above all else, every business owner should take the time and effort to study carefully all location opportunities to determine what is available and which of these choices is best suited to the company's special needs. Remember, no two businesses are exactly alike. No two businesses have identical location requirements. So you must conduct a thorough analysis of your needs before moving ahead to the next steps.

This procedure is recommended for newly-launched and seasoned entrepreneurs alike. Just because a firm has been operating at an undesirable location for years, does not mean management can not entertain proposals for relocating elsewhere. Quite the contrary. It is sound business practice to constantly review all opportunities for more productive operations. The choice of location is at the top of the list.

What should you look for when choosing a location? Well, years of practical experience show that for a retail business there is just no substitute for a heavy flow of consumer traffic. This is so crucial that even poorly-managed companies often do quite well in the really-prime locations; those that add sound management to the mix are goldmines.

When it comes to consumer traffic, however, there is more to consider than just the head count. We must pay attention to the "demographics"—or the statistical makeup of the consumers in the area. Are they young or old, rich or poor, married or single? These factors have a major impact on the kinds of businesses the consumers will patronize. Locating a rock music record shop in a busy shopping area frequented primarily by senior citizens is like running into that brick wall we mentioned earlier. There is no way the business will take off—it is in the wrong market.

On the other hand, placing a business in a market just right for its products and services may also be a mistake. Why? The market may already be saturated with established competitors selling the same offerings. (Competitors who have built up a loyal following through many years of customer service.) That's a tough nut to crack: it's like starting out with two strikes against you.

So how do you determine if a potential site is a winner or an all-out loser? Well, you can go by hearsay, you can try to spot check the area by personal observation—or you can do it scientifically. Believe it or not, most of the information you need is available free-of-charge, or for very minimal fees, from the U.S. Government.

As part of its work, the Bureau of the Census prepares detailed reports on the demographic makeup of population centers throughout the nation. From these reports, savvy businessmen can glean vital and valuable data which is highly effective for selecting choice business locations.

Small firms can make the best use of census bureau publications on population and housing. Statistical reports in these booklets include the following kinds of data for large and small geographic areas:

  *population figures by sex, race and age
  *types of households
  *numbers of rooms per household
  *presence of appliances such as clothes dryers,
     washers and televisions
  *number of automobiles per household

The census on business further clarifies this market information by providing data on competitive businesses in the area. The census business reports list retail and wholesale firms according to sales volume, the number of employees and sales per merchandise line.

So you see that combined census reports on population, housing and business give you a clear picture of a target community. You have a good idea, in advance, if the residents and competition make the area a suitable place to locate your firm.

Everything you need to know about the availability of census bureau reports is contained in an invaluable little booklet called the *Bureau of Census Catalog*. This lists the bureau's publications and lets you order exactly what you need. Write the Superintendent of Documents, Washington, D.C. 20402. You may also find census publications in your local town or university library.

"Whatever you have to do to get your hands on these publications, it's worth the effort," states Lance O., a major appliance merchant in Ohio. "When my partner and I left Sears after working for that giant outfit as merchandise managers for 12 years, we wanted to start a successful business drawing on the valuable experience we'd gained.

"So we naturally chose appliances—TVs, washers, stereos and the like. We knew we wanted to get into really solid growth areas with substantial shopper traffic and little competition. We knew from the hard-luck stories of others that you don't just stumble into these kinds of markets, so we set out to do some scientific research. We turned to the census reports."

Looking over the census data for the state of Ohio, Lance and partner Dinah found that contrary to their original plans, the ideal locations were outside the major urban areas of Cleveland and Cincinnatti. Census reports indicated that the newest of the suburban areas would be best for their needs.

"In these outlying areas we found a potential goldmine waiting to be tapped," Dinah adds. "The statistics said it all: we found towns with a lot of new housing, young families and high median incomes. Most had appliances, to be sure, but virtually all would need more as their families grew and their homes took shape.

"And best of all, the census on business showed very little competition in the area. We checked out the firms that were listed and found we could beat them off easily with superior products and better pricing."

To make a long story short, Lance and Dinah proved to be a dynamic duo in the often profitable appliance business. In just three years, the partners opened 11 successful stores and passed the $8 million annual sales mark in the process. Although no Sears by a long shot, they were two happy and wealthy entrepreneurs.

"Of course," Lance adds, "there is more to this kind of success than just finding the right locations—but it certainly helps. In the same time our fortunes have been rising, we know of at least six appliance merchants in the inner cities that have had to close their doors for the last time. I shudder to think what would have happened to us if we'd followed our original plans and never given serious consideration to location planning."

A lesson for us all.

PUTTING THE WRONG FOOT FORWARD:
How to make first impressions work for you

There's no two ways about it: first impressions last forever. In business as in social relationships, turn off a person at the first encounter and that's the image they're likely to carry from that day on.

Worse yet, put the wrong foot forward in a business meeting and you may never see the person again. That can be a tough pill to swallow when you are talking about potential customers—good business prospects you lose to the competition simply by making that bad first impression.

And yet it happens all the time. Countless companies lose millions of precious dollars simply by failing to prepare for that crucial first contact with the buying public. All too many entrepreneurs are far too casual about first impressions: they don't recognize the need to score a touchdown the first time they carry the ball.

Where do companies go wrong? Why do so many owners fall victim to the kind of poor first impressions that rob their firms of 10 to 40 percent of potential sales? What can be done to make first impressions work in your favor?

For the most part, first impression problems stem from jumping the gun on business openings. Inexperienced entrepreneurs, eager to get the ball rolling and the register ringing, open the front doors before the business is really ready to service customers smoothly and efficiently. The inevitable result is confusion, chaos and a horde of disgruntled customers unlikely to return for a second try.

The point is, the first few weeks or months of business operations should never be reduced to a practice session. Just like good musicians, owner-managers should practice in private. All the kinks and trouble spots should be ironed out before the opening ribbon is cut. Once the company is center stage, all procedures should be smooth and polished.

The secret to this opening day perfection? Simply devoting two full days prior to the opening to rehearsing every aspect of the company's operations. From mail orders to merchandising, from cash control to credit cards, all should be practiced over and over again until employees and management know the systems cold.

The trick is to hold full-scale rehearsals, duplicating all the ingredients of an actual business day. Employees should pose as customers, buying merchandise, exchanging cash and making complaints. This is the only way to assure that the firm is really ready for the challenges of daily business operations.

Failure to take this precaution can be devastating. When a new frozen yogurt shop opened recently in Westchester, N.Y., management sought to cash in on the latest food craze sweeping the nation. Problem is, the store alienated as many people in the first few days of business as most companies do in a lifetime. The reason: completely unprepared for the real world, the owners never anticipated what they would face. The store ran out of yogurt several times, waitresses quit during peak lunch hours and dirty dishes piled up along the counter. Bad word of mouth about the place spread so fast that many potential customers never even gave it a try.

Disasters like this can be avoided by preparing and living by an opening day checklist. Go through the following checks before greeting a single customer:

1. Be certain a key individual is assigned to supervise all non-

management employees. Even if the staff numbers five or less, the delegation of supervisory authority is essential.

2. Carefully instruct all employees in the full scope of their responsibilities. Make sure they know, in advance, how to handle virtually every contingency likely to arise from opening day on.

3. For this initial period only, stock up on more inventory than you think you will need. A good rule of thumb is to overstock by 15 percent more than your sales projections for the period indicate. The reason for this excess stock is clear: run out of goods in the first few weeks or months and you'll turn off potential customers—perhaps lose them forever. Feature a plentiful supply, on the other hand, and you'll earn a reputation for variety and service that will generate positive word-of-mouth so critical to success in the early stages. (Once the business is running on an even keel you'll able to more accurately align inventories to projected demand.)

4. Never open the doors until your entire facility shines from top to bottom. Although it may seem like an elementary precaution, many owner-managers open for business with sloppy, dirty or unfinished facilities. This is unprofessional, unbusinesslike and totally unacceptable to the public. Consumers will not patronize shoddy companies—period!

5. Test all procedures for handling customer complaints. Make sure that every gripe comes quickly and directly to the owner-manager's attention. This kind of responsive mechanism builds excellent customer relations, reduces the likelihood of negative publicity and gets the company off to a good clean start. What's more, it is wise to pay attention to constructive criticism. This is often the best way to discover exactly what your company is doing wrong. Listen to your customers from the start—they are your bread and butter.

6. Practice. Practice. Practice. As we have already mentioned, there is simply no better way to prepare for the rigors of actual business operation than to rehearse for opening day well before the ribbon is ever cut. The old cliche is as true today as it ever was: *"Practice makes perfect."* Remember it.

BITING OFF MORE THAN YOU CAN CHEW: How "positioning" can make you a marketing sharpshooter

Remember the old adage: "You can fool all of the people some of the time, and some of the people all of the time, but you can never fool all of the people all of the time."

The saying is as true today in business as it ever was in politics. It's really very simple: regardless of your product or service, you simply can not be everything to everybody. As a small business you must limit your appeal to a specific market or type of consumer—and then milk that market for all it is worth.

It all boils down to a matter of "business marksmanship." Making it big in today's highly competitive markets demands focusing your efforts on developing a strong, clear and consistent identity for specific groups of consumers. This identity helps to make you a marketing sharpshooter, able to pinpoint your sales targets and pick them off with great accuracy.

The big corporations call this process "positioning." The idea is to distinguish your company from the competition by stressing the unique selling points such as special products, shop-at-home service, low prices and the like. This way you cater to specific market segments (such as senior citizens interested in shop-at-home plans and teenagers looking for trendy fashions) and are in the best position to win their business. You take careful aim on the choicest markets, set your targets and move in for the kill.

The problem is, small companies often display their inexperience by taking just the opposite approach. Rather than setting their sights on an identifiable group of consumers, many owner-managers opt for universal appeal: to shoot for the poor and the affluent, the young and the old, the mod and the conservative. They simply bite off more than they can chew.

Although this shotgun approach may sound wise at first (the larger the potential market the greater the potential sales), the first impression is really deceptive. By going after a widely diverse market, the business is actually limiting rather than expanding its sales potential. The firm will have little expertise in any single market, will have little credibility and will generate a strong appeal to very few consumers. Remember, the wider the range of targets, the greater the likelihood of missing them all. By going after the whole pie, you may wind up without a single slice.

Here's why: building a successful image means building credibility. And you'll never do that by pulling the wool over consumers' eyes. It just won't do to advertise both rock-bottom, bargain basement prices while simultaneously stressing top of the line designer merchandise. Consumers never believe they'll get both in the same outlet—and they are usually right. It is wiser to base a company's appeal on one or the other: prestige merchandise or low prices. That's positioning.

Carol F. of Chappaqua, N.Y. learned the lesson the hard way. When she opened a woman's clothing shop in this affluent suburb of New York, Carol tried to appeal to everyone in town. From fashion-fickle teenagers to aging matrons, Carol stocked merchandise designed to please them all.

The cloudy image problem, however, plagued the new merchant from the start. By catering to such conflicting tastes, Carol's shop never developed a clear image. Was it a trendy boutique? A senior citizens outlet? A haven for lovers of conservative sportswear? Consumers didn't really know—and so they stayed away in droves.

What's more, youngsters were put off by the appeal to older women, and didn't even want to be seen shopping there. Older shoppers, on the other hand, were revolted by the loud stereo music blaring from two over-sized speakers. The shop wasn't their cup of tea, either.

So clearly, we see the magnitude of the problem: by seeking to appeal to everyone, the inexperienced merchant really appeals to no one. The attempt at business expansion actually shrinks market size and sales volume. Fortunately for Carol, a bit of friendly advice helped her to rectify the problem in time to save the shop.

"A neighbor of mine, who happens to work for a local small business consulting group, recognized the mistake I was making. She suggested I concentrate solely on the younger crowd, since a big nearby college might draw hundreds of free-spending, fashion-conscious students.

"I took her advice, and it worked like a charm. I sold off the older women's stock to a jobber and filled in with a hot new line of imported jeans. I even added a juke box to the sales floor and painted the walls in colorful graphics. Best of all, students ate up the image—made the place a hangout—and my sales leaped from $5,000 per month to $32,500."

You too can cash in on the concept of "positioning" by observing the following guidelines to successful image-building:

1. Set your sights on a specific and easily-identifiable market.

2. Avoid the temptation to appeal helter skelter to widely-conflicting consumer groups.

3. Once the target market is identified, "position" your company to develop a close association with that market. Support the positioning strategy with related advertising, merchandising and sales promotion.

4. Be credible. Make a conscious attempt to deliver on your promises. Living up to your image builds valuable word-of-mouth.

5. Continuously gauge the effectiveness of your image through

informal market research. Prepare questionnaires and conduct telephone surveys to determine if your desired image is getting through to consumers.

6. Make a special effort to develop genuine expertise in your market. If you are catering to the teenage population, for example, learn to speak their language, read their magazines and get to know what really turns them on and off. You earn a reputation as an insider—and that's crucial to positioning

PREDICTING SUCCESS PREMATURELY:
How to build a "crystal ball" for your business

As we all know, counting our chickens before they hatch can mean that the chickens will never hatch at all. The reason: jumping the gun on any gradual process can seriously jeopardize the outcome.

This is particularly true in business. Eager to reap the staggering financial rewards of a hot new idea, invention, product or service, many small business people start counting the profits before a single sale is made. Impatience is the demon—and the results can be disastrous.

Professional business management demands an orderly game plan. First the foundation must be laid, then the structure placed in position and finally the finishing touches applied to all the rough edges. Then, and only then, can the venture be considered set and ready to go. Only then can management make any reasonable projections of sales and profits.

Simply guessing at profits without any supporting evidence can spell ruin for even the best of business ideas. That's because any premature prediction of business success can activate a chain reaction of management errors that no company can long sustain.

Take the case of Lila and Amy R. of Brunswick, Maine. The

sisters, school teachers both, dropped out of their profession to open a bookstore near a major university. Since the campus book shop had recently closed due to a disagreement with the student government organization, the sisters believed their store would be a goldmine from day one. After all, there was virtually no competition in sight.

True to form for overconfident, novice entrepreneurs, the sisters went on a spending spree before the shop even opened. They hired contractors to extend the size of the selling floor, purchased lavish fixtures and bought the most sophisticated cash registers and business machines. Based on their rosy projections, the sisters committed to $110,000 in bank debt before they saw a dime in sales.

This chain reaction of spending errors came to haunt them. A week after the sisters' shop opened, student leaders opened their own co-op bookstore on the campus grounds. Suddenly there was serious competition. The goldmine proved to be little more than brass.

Although the sisters were able to compete successfully for a share of the campus book business, the volume was simply inadequate to cover the extraordinary costs incurred to build an overly-large and lavish shop. The sisters were forced to close up in a matter of months; a leaner and simpler operation, free of excess bank debt, could have prospered with the same sales volume.

How to avoid this common mistake? How to predict business performance with some degree of accuracy? How to project a company's profit picture early enough to make some sound management plans?

The answer is simple: build a crystal ball—a crystal ball in the form of a business projection chart designed to gauge the company's likely performance through the coming months and years.

Here's how it works:

*Using private market research or free census department

statistics on your market area, estimate the number of consumers likely to buy from you within the first full month of operation.

*In arriving at this figure, it is generally prudent to consider no more than five percent of potential customers as likely to show any real sales interest and only half that figure to actually conclude a purchase.

*Reduce your estimate of potential sales by five percent for each of the following factors which characterize your firm:

—major competitors in the area

—the strong possibility of new competitors opening up

—your location is in an inconvenient, out-of-the-way area

—you do not plan any initial advertising or sales promotion

*Now you have your final projection for the first full month of operation. You can now extend the projection for the first full year by doing the following:

—Add one percent to the sales projection for every month you stay in business (up to the first 12 months only).

—Boost the base projection by six percent starting the month after you launch a significant and ongoing advertising campaign.

—Boost the base projection by three percent starting the month after you add a major new line of products or services.

Although this chart does not include all of the variables that can affect business performance, it does provide a legitimate starting point for projecting your company's level of success. Feel free to add or subtract percentages if unique conditions not mentioned in the above do characterize your business.

Once the final projection is computed, prospective entrepreneurs have a valuable tool for planning early business decisions. The resulting "crystal ball" can spell out likely sales and profits, and this in turn can provide crucial insights into break-even points, the amount of affordable overhead, and prudent levels of bank borrowing the venture will be able to sustain. The end result is that the company will be better planned and will stand a far greater chance of turning out to be a winner.

That's just what happened to Rick's Pinball Emporium. A winner is the only way to describe a 40-game pinball arcade that has made its 24-year old owner a millionaire in less than two years.

Using the step-by-step projection chart, Rick determined that there would be virtually no market for his arcade for the first six months. That's because a new shopping mall near his arcade was not yet completed and customer traffic in the area would remain slow until the completion date. He had to open up early, however, in order to grab a choice property going for a real bargain price.

Acting on his "crystal ball" findings, Rick pared early expenses to the bone. This way he was able to survive the slow initial months without much business at all. Then, when the mall opened, Rick swung into action. He advertised in all local newspapers, distributed flyers to shoppers visiting the mall, extended his opening hours, and hired a night manager.

The results: three months after the mall opened, Rick's profits were sufficient pay back the loans for each one of the 40 pinball machines. The operation was free and clear and pulling down revenues of $10,000 a month. Now Rick could bask in the glow of success. He was earning at the rate of $100,000 per year and had plans for five more arcades in the works.

A little patience, a little luck and a little planning made it all possible. The former short order cook, with no more than a high school diploma, now lived like a baron in an elegant three-story townhouse on New York's upper east side. He dined at "21", sported about in a sleek, white Jaguar and rode herd over a growing business establishment that churned out money as fast as he could spent it.

What's more, he's one businessman who believes in "crystal balls."

SHUNNING FINANCIAL EXPERTISE:
How to tap the best "money minds"

Of all the complexities of business management, nothing approaches the confusing maze of laws, rules and regulations involved in commercial finance. Unless you are an accountant or economist by training, just the mention of a balance sheet or income statement can send shivers up your spine.

And for good reason. Business finance is not a static science. Constant changes in the tax laws, accounting principles and legal rulings make keeping up with the latest developments a full-time job, a job for highly-trained experts specializing in the art and science of business finance, not for busy owner-managers with little or no financial savvy.

And yet tackling the ins and outs of corporate finance without the proper training is a form of business suicide millions of small business owners practice—and with predictable results. They fail. They fall into bankruptcy and lose substantial investments simply because they are too stubborn to delegate sophisticated functions to those best qualified to do the work.

In today's complex world, the old notion that a small business owner must be a man or woman of "a thousand hats" simply doesn't hold up. Functions like law, accounting and advertising are too sophisticated for laymen to properly handle. To succeed—to avoid the common mistakes—small business must seek out professional advisers. Failure to do so can, and often does, result in overpayment of taxes, inadequate financing, poor cash flow and ignorance of valuable tax shelters.

The best approach, then, is to tap the "money minds." To turn to experts in corporate finance. To utilize professionals best equipped to help you stabilize costs, maximize profits, take advantage of little-known tax breaks and generally tighten control of your operation.

How is this done? Where do you find the "money minds?" How can you get them working for you?

Well, one of the best sources is actually free-of-charge. In most cases, your commercial banker will be more than happy to provide financial consulting services for no more than the cost of keeping an account at the bank. Just relate your goals and problems to the banker, ask for his help, and you'll likely have a knowledgeable new friend in your corner.

Remember, however, that working with bankers and other financial experts is a two-way street. To be successful, you have to do your part to make the relationship work. Here are a few useful tips:

*When choosing a bank, determine if there is a loan officer specializing in small business financing. An officer familiar with small business needs is most likely to be helpful to you.

*Compare a number of area banks to determine which have the widest range of business consulting services. Some banks make it a practice to staff up heavily with local business experts.

*Select a bank with experience in personal financial services for the self-employed such as estate and trust management, automatic savings and bond custody. You'll need all the help you can get with your personal finances as well.

*Invite the banker to your place of business. Be open and candid, revealing everything the officer should know about your operations.

"A banker can never have too much information," says Willis R., one of Detroit's wealthiest and most successful restauranteurs. "The better the officer understands your business, the better the chance of building a good working relationship."

Willis should know. When he opened his first Down Home restaurant, it was the first of its kind in the area with real, old-fashioned home cooking. The place was an instant success and the newly-launched entrepreneur started making big money right off the bat.

Problem was, market research showed that Willis could multiply his profits tenfold by opening four additional Down Home restaurants without delay. The only catch: Willis had not yet amassed nearly enough cash to invest the millions required to build new facilities, furnish them and purchase costly kitchen equipment. He was stymied.

"That, of course, was until I consulted with my banker," Willis adds. "Rather than making the serious blunder of trying to be a know-it-all, I looked to experts for sound advice—and man did it pay off.

"Rather than making huge investments in capital equipment, my banker suggested that I lease the facilities and the equipment. This way I could open up four new outlets at once and cover the costs of the leases with incoming revenues. The plan worked like a charm. Within six months I had five restaurants filled to capacity almost 24 hours a day—and that translated into sales of more than $3½ million per year. For the first time in my life I was really rich—and you can bet that I loved it. What's more, thanks to a buy-back provision the banker built into my leases, I was able to purchase the facilities outright in no time at all. Soon I didn't owe a dime to a soul."

Bankers are only one of the excellent sources of good financial information. For specific problems, try turning to your local Small Business Administration counselors, the accounting department of nearby universities or to an area office of SCORE (Service Corps of Retired Executives).

For year-round advice, accountants are your best source. They can be especially helpful in limiting your taxes to the lowest legal amount. One caution, however: never simply hunt for an accountant in the yellow pages. Give some careful thought and consideration to selecting a well-qualified professional to oversee this most crucial part of your business. There are as many incompetent, lazy and unethical accountants as there are first-class professionals.

Make sure you choose the latter. Ask for recommendations from trade associations, banks and business associates. Choosing a qualified accountant is too important a task to leave to chance.

POOR CREDIT PLANNING:
How to use borrowing power in your business

Let's get one thing straight from the start: borrowing money is not a sign of business weakness—not a last-ditch step to save an otherwise hopeless venture. This old-fashioned view of things has no place in today's sophisticated business environment.

Borrowing is a crucial vehicle for business growth. For small businesses, borrowing is both a catalyst for expansion as well as a cushion for financial setbacks. In the early years especially, when the company has little reserve funds, borrowing can be an indispensable tool for building the company into a solid and profitable venture.

The benefits of borrowing are clear:

*Borrowed capital can yield more than it costs. If you have a sound idea or a going business, the rate of interest will likely be less than the rate of return you can expect to earn from the borrowed funds. So putting borrowed funds to work can be very profitable.

*Interest payments on business borrowing are tax deductible. So Uncle Sam actually subsidizes part of the costs of your borrowing.

*Borrowing is more flexible than ownership. By not tieing

up all of your own funds in business transactions, you maintain a continuous pool of liquid assets. This way the company can take advantage of short-term opportunities and can utilize a source of reserve emergency funds.

   *Loans are generally easier to attract than equity or investment funds. In small companies especially, the likelihood of profits is too uncertain to encourage most investment capital. Lenders are more willing to put up money because they have prior claims to income and assets.

   This is not to suggest, however, that borrowing is easy. Quite the contrary—and that is the essential point. Borrowing money requires proving to a potential lender that you and your company are good prospects—that you are likely to be successful enough the repay the loan. You'll have to instill trust, present a strong case and do a considerable amount of advance planning.

   Planning is perhaps the most crucial step of all—and yet it is the action most small business owners ignore. If there is a classic of all common business mistakes, this is it. The reason is clear: the failure to establish good lines of credit exposes small firms to financial strangulation at the very times the money is needed most. That is what the "house of cards syndrome" is all about. Building a successful venture without sound credit planning can result in the entire structure caving in at the very first business setback.

   Credit planning is vital for one major reason: lenders want to know of you and your business before you need to borrow money. The chances of running in off the street and obtaining an emergency business loan from your local bank or finance company are slim. Successful borrowing demands developing, in advance, a sound working relationship with potential lenders. It means letting a bank or other lending organization know something about your company (its method of operations, profit projections, past history, etc) even before you want to borrow money. This is the way to establish your company as a viable commercial venture worthy of business loans.

   This way, when the money is needed most, you have the best

chance of obtaining it. Why? Because you are a known quantity. The lender knows you and your business and can use this knowledge to hedge his risks. This is central to the way bankers think and operate.

Sandi K's diligence in planning for credit sources paid off big when she needed a quick infusion of cash to tide her over an unexpected slump in sales. When the orders for her new line of women's sportswear dropped by 40 percent from the year earlier, Sandi was close to panic. The ten years of painstaking work in building her company SUPERWEAR into a major force in New York's garment industry seemed in jeopardy.

But being the tough entrepreneur that she was, Sandi kept her head, did a little research, and found that a few style changes would be all that was necessary to sign up a giant department store and thereby put her over the top. Her short-term need, however, was to get some cash borrowing going to cover payroll and other costs until sales started climbing.

No problem. For years Sandi worked very closely with a business banking specialist at a nearby branch of a leading New York bank. The result: a brief explanation of her needs produced a check for $56,000. The whole process was quick and painless. More important, Sandi avoided the "house of cards sydrome," kept the roof from caving in, revised her sportswear line, and wound up with record annual sales of $1.9 million. A great year. A smart businesswoman.

You can be just as smart. Start building up your credit sources now. Use the following strategy to make you a successful borrower:

1. Try to deal with a single commercial bank for all your business banking needs. Working with more than one bank divides your loyalties and dilutes your clout.

2. Work with a banker well in advance of your borrowing needs. Involve the banker in your basic business planning.

3. Work only with those banks with a history of making small business loans. Knowledge of small business needs and problems is often crucial for obtaining adequate funding. (A good way to

gauge this is to determine if the bank has a small business lending officer.)

4. Enquire about opening a line of credit. If you qualify, this kind of arrangement can guarantee you instant money whenever it is needed (up to the maximum amount established).

5. Make a contact at the Small Business Administration. Let local SBA officials know of you and your company now, so that lending may be more likely in the future. Remember, SBA funding is often at subsidized interest rates, well below those charged by commercial banks.

(For the address of the nearest SBA office write the Small Business Administration, Washington, D.C.)

6. Also write the SBA for a list of Small Business Investment Corporations. SBICs are government chartered financial organizations established to fund small businesses (especially minority-owned companies).

INADEQUATE CASH RESERVES:
How to beat business enemy number one

More than ever before, the business of business is money: how to make it, stretch it, spend and invest it. With capital supplies short and inflation rates high, the drive to make the most of the business buck has never been greater.

This emphasis on productive use of business funds is strongest in the early stages of business development. New companies, after all, have no time to waste. Locked in a race against time and competition, newly launched firms must make profitable use of invested capital without delay. Every management decision must be geared to one overriding objective: to make money make money. To get the ball rolling and generate sufficient revenues to cover initial expenses. All new ventures need time to breath—time to grow and develop as mature and profitable businesses.

Money buys this time. Money the company earns in its earliest days and, even more important, money that management invests up front to get the firm off the ground. This "up front" investment is crucial both to the company's chances for survival and, better yet, its eventual success.

The fact is this: most small companies fail, in part, because there is too little money up front. The ventures are under-capitalized and the reason for this is usually clear: in the mad race to start making big money, inexperienced entrepreneurs rush out and open the doors before there is enough money in the bank to see the firm through the tough sledding of its early days.

After all, very few companies have that ideal combination of products and services that prompts customers to beat down the doors the day the business opens. Quite the contrary. Even the greatest money-making businesses of all time have required time to learn the ropes, earn a reputation and build solid customer support. To repeat, money buys this time. Money pays for the rent, labor, utilities and materials needed to keep the company afloat until the big dollars start flooding in.

But how much is enough? How much reserve cash is required to launch a small business? How much reserve is needed to cover early expenses and to generate initial revenues?

Although the exact amount of investment differs for every commercial venture, general guidelines can be followed to help avoid the common mistake of inadequate reserves. Use the following formula to gauge your ideal cash pool:

*Compute the total of all fixed costs likely to be incurred in the first 16 months of operation. Fixed costs are those which remain constant regardless of the level of business activity. This includes rent, insurance, basic utilities, and major equipment.

*Figure the total of all variable costs you'll likely face during this same 16 month period. Variable costs are those which move up or down with business activities and include such items as labor, advertising, raw materials, and processing.

*Use market research to project the number of customers you are likely to service in the first 16 months. Multiply this figure by the average dollar amount of goods they are likely to purchase. This second computation will provide your raw revenue projection. Once you have established the figure, reduce it by 25 percent. It is more than likely that your customer number and dollar amount projections are too high and need adjustment now. It is better to be safe than sorry.

*Add the total of all projected fixed and variable costs for the first 16 months. Now increase this figure by 30 percent. Chances are you figured costs too low, ignored the inflation factor, left out key items or failed to set aside reserves for unexpected emergencies. This is the reason for the 30 percent adjustment.

*Now, for the crucial step, compare the figures for adjusted revenue projections with adjusted total cost projections. If projected costs exceed anticipated revenues, hold off on launching the business until more capital can be found. If this is impossible, take steps to reduce initial costs so that they are substantially below adjusted revenue projections. This can be done by searching for lower-rent facilities, cutting the work force, etc. (Note: In this discussion, up front capital refers to cash required to absorb the difference between revenues and expenses and is aside from cash required for building facilities, purchasing equipment, etc.)

*One extra precaution. If projected costs and revenues are neck and neck, boost up front capital by 15 percent before launching the business. It is always advisable to prepare in advance rather than sweating it out for more cash once the company's very life is on the line.

This formula is useful as a general guideline for new businesses and for established companies planning branch offices or new product lines. Harry B. used it quite successfully when planning the opening of a chain of discount record stores in and around Los Angeles.

Already an established entrepreneur—owner of Home-World, a huge home furnishings emporium—Harry knew full well the risks and the tremendous opportunities in running a personal business. So when he recognized the lucrative potential in the retail record business, he set out to grab off some of the profits—but only after carefully planning his capital needs. He did not want to have to give up his money-making idea in midstream for lack of sufficient capital—and, worse yet, he did not want the record business to drain the already highly profitable HomeWorld.

The solution: Harry and his accountant computed a projected cost and revenue analysis for SoundWorld's (the record store chain) first 16 months of operation. The figures looked like this:

Projected total revenues for six SoundWorld stores: $2,122,000. Projected total costs (fixed and variable—adusted): $2,052,000.

"The computation indicated that our SoundWorld stores would be only marginally profitable in the first 16 months of business—the time it would take to adequately promote the company and attract teenagers with our discount prices," Harry said. "So we knew that in planning our bank financing agreements, we should obtain at least $250,000 more in reserve funds than we initially assumed would be necessary. This would provide the extra cushion required, especially in the first six months (when losses would be heaviest). By computing our cost and revenue projections on a monthly basis, we knew exactly how much extra cash we needed to stay solvent until the business picked up and paid for itself." The planning proved to be both a life saver—and a money maker.

"Although five of our new stores performed better than our projections," Harry explains, "one was a real loser from the start. We had no choice but to cut our losses at that location and close it up after six months. This meant unexpected expenses in legal fees, lease transactions and the like. Luckily, we had built in the reserve funds and were able to meet the problem head on.

"We bit the bullet, closed down the loser and concentrated on our other five successful outlets. And, just as we expected, they all started churning out the heavy profits after about 18 months of operations. Suddenly, the revenue curve left the cost figures in the dust and we were riding the crest of one of the most successful new retail ventures in the L.A. area in decades."

The numbers speak for themselves: by the close of the fourth year, SoundWorld stores boasted 36 outlets with annual revenues of $18.4 million: pre-tax profits of $4.1 million. As sole owner, Harry raked in the rewards. He was rich, smart, happy and semi-retired by his 50th birthday.

What a way to celebrate!

BEING A SOFT TOUCH ON BAD DEBTS:
How to use the secret of super credit

When it comes to profitable business ownership, there is simply no room for the "soft touch." Learning to lend money to only the most reliable borrowers is lesson number one for many an owner-manager.

Regardless of your generosity in personal life, when it comes to business the rules of business must rule. All too many entrepreneurs have watched as once-prosperous ventures drowned helplessly in a sea of red ink—drowned in a flood of uncollectible bills. Basing lending decisions on chance or friendship can make this happen to the most vital of firms. It can happen to yours.

Building a successful small business, in fact, means learning what big business has known for years. That is that extending business credit is a crucial yet delicate service: handle it right and it multiplies business many times over; treat it casually and it returns like a boomerang with damaging force.

Unfortunately, "seat of the pants" credit procedures are the rule, not the exception, for most small businesses. Accustomed to informal operations based on personal instincts, many owner-managers lend money this way too. They are a "soft touch" for every con artist, flim flam man, free loader and poor credit risk in the area. More often than not, those rejected by large corporations' sophisticated credit procedures are later accepted by small business. And small business winds up the loser.

Why is the proper management of business credit so important? Simply because poor credit practices cost small businesses billions of dollars per year. Money down the drain because owner-managers extend credit to virtually every applicant. Money the company might have turned into bottom line profits but instead winds up as nothing more than a figure on a delinquent accounts report.

The failure to adapt tough and uniform credit practices simply cheats a business of its true potential, deprives the owner of maximum profits and increases the risks of financial crisis. The answer, obviously, is to get tough with credit decisions today!

The problem is more than a matter of honesty. Delinquent accounts weigh like a ball and chain on a company's finances. Disruptions in cash flow, for example, interfere with the firm's ability to pay its bills, order merchandise or expand operations. As a result, management is forced into high-interest bank borrowing to take up the slack.

What can be done to prevent these problems? How can management avoid the mistakes so common to credit transaction? In today's credit-oriented society, simply refusing to grant any credit at all is not the answer. Millions of consumers, industrial purchasing agents and distributors rely on one type of credit or another to acquire needed products and services. This ranges from credit cards to company charge accounts to extended payment plans. Virtually every business in operation today must offer at least one of these plans or risk the threat of losing a significant percentage of prime customers to the competition. Remember, credit, if handled properly, is an extraordinary business booster, capable of expanding sales by 100 percent or more. The goal then is to maximize the benefits of business credit while simultaneously reducing the risks.

This seemingly utopian objective can actually be accomplished without magic, luck or arm-twisting. All you have to do is set up a rigorous and uniform system of credit screening for all existing and potential customers. And this screening must be up front—accomplished before a single dollar of credit is extended to a single individual or company.

The idea is to ascertain that all potential borrowers are the kind of people, or companies, with good track records for prompt bill paying. Numerous credit studies reveal that for the most part those who pay their bills promptly do so all the time; those who are delinquent with one account are usually in bad standing with a number of creditors. The solution then is to weed out the habitual free loaders from the start—to reduce the risks of credit losses by refusing to grant credit to those customers with a poor credit history. This approach assures the best of both worlds: you enjoy the goodwill and patronage of credit worthy customers and identify the bad risks before they can get their hooks in you. It's like having your cake and eating it too. Who says that can't be done?

Use the following procedures to verify customer credit before allowing a dime's worth of goods or services to go unpaid:

*Prepare an index card file. At the time an applicant applies for credit, make out a card for the individual and jot down the following information: name, address, employer, bank names and account numbers, and names of other (three) credit sources for references.

*Verify all information, paying particular attention to the credit references of other lenders including department store charge departments, credit card companies and banks.

*Deny credit if there is any evidence at all of habitual poor payment practices, bankruptcies or legal action. Note the card as such and keep for future reference.

*Extend credit in cases where all references and other information appear satisfactory. It is crucial, however, to maintain active surveillance of each and every authorized credit account. Review all payment records on a monthly basis, constantly weeding out those who are slow or delinquent before they have the opportunity to go bad on a very large account.

*Avoid extending credit to friends or family members. It is difficult to be objective with closely-related borrowers—and this leaves open the biggest opportunity for credit abuses. It is surprising how many healthy companies go down the drain for the simple mistake of placing too much trust in loved ones.

If a poor risk sneaks through your credit screening system, as will happen from time to time, the next phase of sophisticated credit practices is to call in experts to help collect on bad accounts. Never make the common mistake of trying to be your own collection agency.

For most small firms, the burden of bad debt is best handled by professional collection agencies. As specialists in the function, agencies are well-equipped to deal with the evasive practices of delinquent accounts.

"Very often, a dunning letter on our letterhead will pry loose a stubborn account," says Guy Knight, a senior vice president of Dunn & Bradstreet's commercial collection division. "It's a psychological phenomenon. The debtor sees that a collection agency is involved and then realizes that the creditor means business. This recognition can be just the thing to prompt immediate payment."

How can small companies select and hire competent collection agencies? What are standard fees? What can be expected in terms of the agency-client relationship?

The following guidelines, developed by experts in the field, cover agency costs and procedures and suggest steps clients can take to facilitate the collection process:

1. As a general rule, accounts more than 90 days past due should be turned over to a collection agency. Ninety days is the maximum reasonable waiting period for most accounts.

2. The earlier an account is handed over for collection, the better the chances of obtaining payment. Accounts delinquent for one year or more are exceptionally difficult to collect and may, in fact, be refused by many agencies.

3. Most agencies use a three-part procedure to collect on

delinquent accounts. Dunning letters graduate to personal contact, and, if still unsuccessful, to legal action.

4. In most cases, agency fees are levied only if the delinquent account is paid. Fees range from 15 percent of the settlement all the way up to 50 percent. The general rule states that the smaller the transaction, the higher the fee.

5. Prospective clients should shop around for a competent agency. It is accepted practice to request a list of the agency's clients and to check out its reputation with business or trade groups. This is the best way to gauge the agency's performance.

6. Many collection agencies offer a useful service known as "free demand." Under the terms of the service, the agency will write a dunning letter to debtors requesting that delinquent funds be paid. If payment is made within ten days of the letter, there is no charge for the agency's service.

7. Companies can reduce their intake of rubber checks by demanding dual identification and by refusing to accept "starter checks." Checks with no printed name or address are often used for fraudulent purposes.

8. The processing of a delinquent account can take anywhere from ten days to one year or more depending on the size and complexity of the transaction. In most cases, however, the account is settled or given over for legal action within three months.

ACCEPTING RUBBER CHECKS:
How a new service reduces the risk

Unfortunately, the problem of business credit is actually a two-headed monster. For apart from the risks of offering charge accounts and the like, there is the equally troublesome dilemma of what to do with business checks. Once again you face the old problem of being "damed if you do and damned if you don't."

Of all the time-honored plagues of business ownership, few rival the persistence of the "rubber check." In spite of years of advances in credit practices, taking the bounce out of business checks is probably harder now than ever before. That's because in our increasingly cashless society, the check is the prime instrument of business transactions. You have to accept some degree of risk as part of the price of business ownership.

For millions of small businesses, however, dealing with checks is like rolling the dice: every move is a gamble. Accepting checks means inevitable losses from fraud, bankruptcy and inadequate funds. This combination of factors drains the self-employed of billions of hard-earned dollars.

"I was once so naive, that when I think back on it now I can hardly believe it," says St. Louis furniture merchant Armand S. "I used to accept checks from every Tom, Dick and Harry who came into my store with an honest look on his face. It's a wonder I'm still in business today.

"The problem is especially acute when you are selling big-ticket items like furniture, tires, carpeting, suits and the like. Customers don't want to carry around big wads of cash and many refuse to use credit cards. So you either accept personal checks or say good-bye to a lot of good business. In most cases, you wind up taking checks rather than losing out to the competition.

"When a check turns out to be rubber, however, the loss is usually quite heavy. In the big-ticket trades it's not unusual to write a sale of several thousand dollars. Losses like that turn a lot of your profits into sand."

Armand speaks from experience. A casual check cashing policy wound up costing this otherwise intelligent merchant more than $178,000 in dead and uncollectible checks before he got smart and put an end to carte blanche check cashing.

"First, I refused to cash any third-party checks. This increases the likelihood of foul play and makes it increasingly difficult to collect when the checks are returned unpaid. What's more, any checks with crossed out numbers or suspicious-looking signatures were also rejected right off the bat. There's no sense asking for trouble and a few simple precautions like these can make all the difference between accepting or rejecting obviously rubber checks. In my case, it cut my losses in half almost immediately."

Then Armand really got smart. He searched for a system of really risk-free check cashing—the answer to every owner-manager's headaches—and he found it. So can you.

"We think we are the answer," says George J. Warner, a sales broker for Telecredit—a national check cashing credit service. "Telecredit is designed with the small business owner in mind. It enables the self-employed to accept most checks with no financial risk at all. By doing so, the service protects those firms least able to sustain a bad credit experience."

Similar to major credit card programs, Telecredit features both computerized credit analyses and payment guarantees to subscribing businesses. The twin benefits to Telecredit users are the removal of credit risks and the assurance of prompt payment.

"A look at a typical case shows how fast and simple our service is," Warner adds. "Let's say the owner of a retail tire shop has the chance to sell a set of radials to an out-of-town motorist. Problem is, the potential customer wants to pay by check. Should the merchant accept the credit risk?

"With Telecredit, there's no need to worry. The merchant simply calls our toll-free telephone number, gives the customer's name and driver's license number, and obtains authorization to cash the check in a matter of seconds. If approval is granted and the check turns out to be bad, the retailer is covered for the full amount up to a maximum of $600."

Although the vast majority of checks are reportedly approved on the spot by the Telecredit operators, a small precentage are deemed unacceptable. Even in these cases, however, customers may speak with Telecredit supervisors to explain unfavorable credit information. This may lead to a reversal of the initial decision and full authorization to cash the check.

Telecredit subscribers are protected against covered losses by so-called "forgery bonds." These documents call for prompt reimbursement, by an insurance company, for all authorized checks returned unpaid to Telecredit subscribers.

On the negative side, Telecredit's protective service is costly. The basic fee is four percent of the face amount of all authorized checks. For checks of $18.50 or less, the charge is 75 cents per check—and there is a $5 monthly minimum fee for every subscriber.

Telecredit subscribers are not required, however, to pass along all incoming checks through the approval system. Owner-managers may limit their use of the Telecredit service to approvals for those checks with high-risk potential. This selective process circumvents the four percent fee for "safe" checks.

"Any way you slice it, Telecredit helps small companies boost their sales," Warner claims. "That's because there's rarely ever a need to turn away a customer. Our toll-free numbers are manned around the clock—seven days a week—so credit can be checked at any time. What's more, we authorize checks from any state in the country. It's like blanket credit protection for checks."

Owner-managers interested in learning more about Telecredit may check the yellow pages for the name of the nearest sales agent or contact Telecredit at 1901 Avenue of the Stars, Los Angeles, CA, 90067. Toll-free telehone: 800-421-0839.

Combined with your own system of screening personal checks, Telecredit's service may be just the thing to keep your business protected from the threat of the "rubber check."

IGNORING FINANCIAL STATISTICS: How an ounce of prevention can keep your business strong

Whether you are a newly-launched or a seasoned entrepreneur, you know there is considerable excitement in running your own business—a thrill you simply cannot achieve working for someone else. You are a manager, an investor, a wheeler-dealer—and you're proud of it all.

The problem is, this pride and excitement can, and often does, turn the owner's attention from the basics. And in business, *numbers* are the basics. Regardless of your proficiency in drumming up sales, the company will never amount to much unless you know where you stand on balance sheets, bank accounts, profit ratios and productivity.

It is quite common for once-prosperous companies to return to sand simply because owner-managers make the common mistake of ignoring financial statistics. The feeling is that math should be left to the mathematicians; finances saved for accountants. The flaw in this thinking is that it is only partially correct. Although complex matters should be left to the experts, every business owner should be familiar with the basic concepts of commercial finance. It is the only way to keep tabs on your business where it really counts: at the roots.

The essential point is that financial statistics are key business indicators. They serve as warning lights, alerting owners to possible deep-seated problems developing far below the tip of the iceberg. Knowing how to look for these warning lights makes it possible for you to spot troubles in the early stages—when they are simpler and easier to correct. This helps to keep the business strong and reduces the likelihood of severe financial crises. One of the nation's leading business managers—the chief executive of a multi-billion dollar giant—calls this the policy of "no surprises." It means always knowing enough about your business to control it from the bottom up.

What should you know? At the very least, you should be familiar with the following: balance sheets, profit and loss statements, sales to profit ratios, backlog, depreciation, accounts receivables, debt financing and asset-productivity ratios.

Knowledge of these statements and formulas can help you keep tabs on your businesses from the inside out. You'll know, for example, how much a new piece of equipment will likely return to you in extra profits. Or how much you'll have to boost sales in order to boost net income by 20, 30 or 40 percent. This data can be crucial when you are amassing cash for lucrative business opportunities.

You'll find all you need to know about the basics in a series of handy little guides published by the Small Business Administration. Just write to your local SBA office and ask for a checklist on small business financial publications. Most of the booklets are available to you free. Take the time to read them.

In addition, you can work with a helpful formula which can be used to monitor your company's performance on a regular basis. Why not grab a spare notebook and jot down how the formula works.

Remember, your goal, at all times, is to earn a profit. If you are not, something is basically wrong with your operation. You must get back on the track—and you must do it fast. Most often, this requires taking a close look at the financial statistics which reveal the most about your business.

An excellent technique for doing this is to develop a "break-even chart." This mathematical device can tell precisely where you stand in dollars and cents. By indicating your company's break-even volume (the point at which you neither lose nor make money), the chart illustrates exactly how much management will have to boost sales to generate substantial profits—to put the business firmly in the black.

Here's how it is done. Break-even volume equals the sum of your total fixed costs (costs which do not vary with the level of business activity) divided by the selling price, minus the variable cost per unit of merchandise you sell. It looks like this:

$$\text{Break-even volume} = \frac{\text{total fixed costs}}{\text{selling price-variable cost per unit}}$$

Using real figures, let's take the case of the Rooth Corporation. The firm figures the costs for one of its products as follows: total fixed costs, $100,000; variable cost, $50 per unit. This means that $50 per unit can be applied towards fixed costs. With fixed costs of $100,000, 2,000 units will have to be sold before any profit is earned. From that point on, after fixed costs are recovered, the $50 per unit sold will be profit.

The break-even point of 2,000 units is figured as such:

$$\text{Break-even volume} = \frac{\$100,000}{\$100-\$50} = 2,000$$

By exploring this hard financial data, the management of the Rooth Corporation knows precisely how many units of each of its products it must sell to earn a profit. There is no guessing— no seat of the pants approximations involved.

"When we determine that profits are not being earned on a particular product, we quickly make up a break-even chart to determine if inadequate sales is the problem," says company president and owner Al Rooth. "We don't make the tragic mistake of trying to guess our way out of a jam—that's just not accurate enough for today's sophisticated business world.

"What's more, by gauging the break-even point, we know what kind of sales figures we have to shoot for way before any trouble ever sets in. This keeps us healthy, rich and way ahead of the competition."

A word to the wise: prepare a break-even analysis for all of your company's product and service lines. You'll have a better understanding of your business; tighter controls; a more accurate target for sales drives; and an effective aid in tracking down trouble spots. What more can you ask?

THE CRISIS OF INSUFFICIENT FUNDS:
How to keep your company "liquid"

There is more to good-sense financial management than simply keeping tabs on break-even performance. The list of key business indicators you can monitor runs into the hundreds.

We do not, however, expect you to know and use each and every one of them. First, you are most likely a financial layman: some of the more complex indicators are simply over your head. What's more, as a busy owner-manager you don't have the time to devote hour after hour to intricate mathematical formulas.

To make life easier for you, we have isolated those few indicators so crucial to your business that you must take the time to understand and utilize them. There is just no two ways about it: in today's complex world, some things are absolutely necessary to the management of a successful business.

These key indicators all relate to the concept of "liquidity." Whether you understand this concept or not, pay attention. It is a lesson you can never learn well enough. Failure to prepare for adequate liquidity is a serious business blunder—one of the major causes of cash crises.

Put simply, liquidity is the ability to pay your bills. It is a prime objective of financial management. Liquidity answers the question "Does the company have enough cash, plus assets that can be readily turned into cash, so that it can pay all debts that will come due during the present accounting period?"

The failure to keep your company sufficiently liquid will result in an inability to pay the firm's bills. This is the best way to bring on the crisis of insufficient funds—to back yourself into a corner and permanently damage your business.

You can work to avoid this dangerous predicament by testing the company's liquidity on a regular basis. Set aside a notebook for this very purpose and jot down the following formulas for your use:

*The *current ratio* is one of the most highly-regarded and oft-used measures of financial strength. It is computed from balance sheet data by dividing the company's current assets by its current liabilites.

For example, the ABC Manufacturing Company, with current assets of $140,000 and current liabilities of $60,000 has a current ratio of 2.3 to 1.

This is figured as such:

$$\frac{\text{Current assets}}{\text{current liabilities}} = \frac{\$140,000}{\$60,000} = 2.3 \text{ (or 2.3 to 1)}$$

By most standards in use today, this ratio of 2.3 to 1 is considered good. Two to one or better is usually deemed sufficient to keep the company solvent even in spite of minor setbacks or brief downturns. To be cautious managers, however, we suggest that you strive for an ever greater margin of safety: a ratio of three to one or better. Giving your firm an extra financial cushion to absorb the unexpected shocks is, after all, one of the best ways to avoid the common mistakes which kill off so many businesses.

*An even more exacting measure of liquidity than the current ratio is the *acid test ratio*. This is considered a highly-precise measure because it excludes inventories and focuses on the really liquid assets.

The acid test ratio is computed as follows:

$$\frac{\text{cash} + \text{government securities} + \text{receivables}}{\text{current liabilities}}$$

For ABC Manufacturing, which has no government securities, the total of cash and receivables is $70,000; the liabilities remains at $60,000. So we have:

$$\frac{\$70,000}{\$60,000} = 1.2 \text{ to } 1$$

An acid test ratio of 1 to 1 is considered satisfactory providing the company is in solid financial condition with little threat of receivables problems. Hard to collect receivables can, of course, seriously impair the firm's liquidity. Once again we suggest that you aim for an extra margin: an acid test ratio of 2 to 1.

Keep in mind that liquidity is not an idle measurement of abstract business performance. It is a central business indicator, revealing the company's ability to pay its bills. The failure to keep tabs on liquidity can bring on bankruptcy in a flash. Small companies especially do not have the resources to sustain longstanding setbacks unless adequate provisions were made in advance. So learn from others' mistakes—from the thousands of companies that go bankrupt every year. Do all you can to keep your company liquid.

You can improve your company's liquidity by taking any or all of the following steps:

1. Increase your current assets with loans or other borrowing.

2. Increase your current assets by adding equity, preferably cash, to the business. There's no better way to build in a good financial cushion that to maintain solid cash reserves in an interest-paying account.

3. Plow more of your profits back into the venture. Don't be so quick to pay out earnings, regardless of the temptations. First make sure you have covered the home base by building in a solid base of liquid assets.

PRACTICING ABSENTEE OWNERSHIP:
How to make sure of your personal control

"Good guys finish last."

There's a lot of truth in old cliches—and this one is right on the money. For when it comes to running a business venture, popularity has little to do with success. Being a good guy, in fact, often means you'll wind up on the losing end of the stick.

What does this mean? Simply that all too many business owners make the oft-repeated mistake of trying to be a friend to their employees. Although this may sound very nice and commendable, it is not a wise strategy at all. Why? Because the owner is not the employees' friend—he is their boss. And unless this is spelled out clear and strong from the start, the owner will wind up a victim of his own policies.

It all boils down to a matter of trust. Choosing to be an "absentee owner," and allowing employees to run the business without direct supervision, is a sure way to invite employee fraud, theft and general carelessness. No matter how well you know the people working for you, and regardless of their talents and abilities, you simply cannot trust others to run your business for you. Only you care enough to do it right.

And yet it happens time and again that small business

owners, for one reason or another, opt for the easy way out: absentee ownership. Rather than giving the firm the kind of hard work and dedication every business requires from its owner, these half-hearted entrepreneurs prefer to spend their time at the golf course or the tennis courts. They want the best of both worlds: ownership of a successful business and a life of leisure. Although this can be managed in the later stages of business success, it is virtually impossible in the formative years when the company is growing from the ground up.

Those entrepreneurs who shoot for absentee ownership must place all of their faith and trust in employees. For it is employees who are actually left to run the business while the owner is teeing off on the ninth hole.

"When I think back on how I tried to run my business from the deck of my pleasure boat, I shudder," says Dale N., president of a huge plumbing supply house near Phoenix, Arizona. "Once I got the business going, I wanted to wash my hands of the work and leave that to others.

"So I took the nice guy approach. I told my workers—sales clerks, stock boys, managers and all—that I trusted them to keep things running smoothly. I emphasized my respect for their abilities and stressed that I wouldn't be looking over their shoulders to check on their progress. I promised not to treat them like children."

To make a long story short, Dale's nice-guy approach, typical of the common mistake so many owners make, backfired on him. And backfired in a big way.

"One afternoon I was home having some drinks around the pool when my banker called me. He told me that my main corporate account was overdrawn by $11,000—even though the records my employees prepared for me showed a balance of $22,380.

"Well, that proved to be only the tip of the iceberg. By the time I took the first good look at my company that I'd taken in two years, I found that I'd been bilked out of $73,000. Worse yet, my major accounts were fed up with the way the business was being run and several were threatening to buy elsewhere. My company was in shambles—and I was to blame."

That was the end of absentee ownership for Dale. No more

Mr. Nice Guy at business, he now runs a tight ship on the job. Boating and swimming are reserved for the weekends—during working hours Dale is at the office calling the shots. He's the boss again—no longer the trusting friend—and his business is strong again for it.

"I'm still nice to my employees, to be sure, but I am around here looking over their shoulders," Dale adds. "This company runs on control now, not friendship, and this has helped me hold on to each and every customer we almost lost. What's more, I'm no longer an easy mark for employee fraud: my bank accounts are in order and the company is making more money than ever before. The next time I leave this company for someone else to run is when I retire."

There are ways, of course, to prevent the pitfalls of absentee ownership without living with a business 24 hours a day. Even the most devoted owner must take time off for vacations, business travel and personal needs. So follow these "Six Steps to Keeping the Boss in Control," and you will help discourage foul play and employee incompetence. You may not be a "good guy," but you stand a better chance of owning a profitable business.

1. Whenever you leave the place of business, for any reason, leave clear information on your destination, length of absence and how you can be reached. Instruct your subordinates to contact you immediately concerning any major business developments. Make it clear that no one is to make decisions for you.

2. Assign a key individual to serve as manager in your absence. Inform all employees of this assignment and demand that all executive matters be brought to this individual's attention when you are not available. This individual is not, in any way, to serve as your replacement. The person simply serves as a focal point for priority matters and centralizes any potential problems in the realm of a single individual. This reduces the likelihood of widespread chaos and loss of cental control. It is up to you, however, to keep close tabs on this person's performance.

3. Never leave your business on a regular basis or for extended periods of time. If a good deal of road work is required, try to delegate this aspect of management to an employee. There is simply no substitute for the owner-manager himself running

things at the actual place of business. Just the presence of authority is usually sufficient to discourage most of the excesses that take place when the boss is an absentee owner.

4. Run periodic checks on your own operations. The best way to determine how your employees are performing is to check on their work—and their honesty—without prior notice.

One good technique is to call the company as if you were a potential customer. See what kind of service you get. Was an all-out effort made to handle your needs? Were the employees courteous and polite?

Also, ask a friend to visit your place of business and make a purchase. Have the individual check to see that all funds are properly rung up and put in the register draw—not the employee's pocket. A simple check like this can save many thousands of dollars.

5. Build in a system of checks and balances into all financial transactions. Insist, for example, that all company checks carry two signatures—one of which, in most cases, should be yours.

Do the same for petty cash reserves, bank transactions and accounts receivable. Make sure that at least two individuals sign for and carefully document every procedure.

Double check all of your safeguards by having your accountant audit all the books on a regular basis. Ask him to review all possible areas of employee fraud.

6. Last but not least, use your ultimate weapon—the power of dismissal—whenever there is any proof of foul play, repeated carelessness or incompetence. As the boss of your business, it is your responsibility to fire those not worthy of being on your payroll.

Firing the bad apples not only rids the firm of its deadweight, but also establishes you as an authority figure. Those engaged in unsavory activities—and those just contemplating them—will think twice when they know there is a strong force on the premises.

You may not be a "good guy," but you won't finish last.

ALLOWING RUNAWAY INVENTORIES:
How to fight off the invisible threat

"The delicate balance." These three words best describe the secret to solving one of the most stubborn problems of business management today: how to control inventories. Take all the mathematical formulas, computer controls and the like used in modern inventory management and behind each and every one you'll find that universal goal of striking "the delicate balance" between supply and demand.

One of the biggest problems here is that all too many business owners fail to recognize the importance of inventory management. Many never even give a thought to what is piled up in the stockroom unless there is a fire or a serious shortage of goods. Inventories are just not considered important.

This seat-of-the-pants approach is wrong. Whether you are just starting out in business, or are a veteran of 30 years or more, you likely face a problem which is as common among the Fortune 500 corporations as among local retail shops. The problem is inventories and the challenge is trying to strike that delicate balance between supply and demand.

And a delicate balance it is. Carrying what is commonly referred to as "bloated inventories" can mean that the business has too much of its cash tied up in merchandise sitting in a back room or company warehouse. In most cases, this capital could be put to more productive use as liquid funds for expansion efforts or simply for cash reserves. No small business can afford the inefficiency of tieing up its cash in excess inventory—pure and simple.

Most important, bloated inventories can produce substantial losses. By going overboard and stocking up on more goods than you can hope to sell, there is a good chance that you will be stuck holding the bag with thousands of dollars of unsold merchandise.

Remember, in our fast-paced world, styles and trends change all the time—and they change rapidly, often without warning. One of the nation's hottest new products—a special bubble gum—recently took off like a rocket, breaking all sales records in the first few months on the market. Then, almost as quickly, sales nosedived due to a silly and unsubstantiated rumor that the product could be unhealthy. Suddenly, a demand product turned into a surplus product. Just think what that does to those who order excess inventories. It means money is sunk into a product that will not sell.

That's just the point: heavy inventories limit your marketing flexibility. Those companies burdened with bloated inventories are committed to selling the products they are stocking. Management can not easily move with the times—can not easily adjust to rapid changes in style and taste. And yet this very flexibility is what small companies must rely on to compete with giant competitors.

In addition, bloated inventories can cost you money by forcing your firm to borrow unnecessarily from banks and other sources at high interest rates. This is a very common mistake repeated over and over again by thousands of small companies.

"When I first started out in business for myself, I paid little or no attention to inventories," admits Sarah L., owner of BusinessProds, an office supply distributor in Chicago. "And man, did I pay the price. When a brand new combination digital clock and pencil sharpener came out, I thought it would be a big winner so I just ordered 10,000 of them—simply because that sounded like a good round number. Anyway, the item was a real dog and I was stuck with $100,000 invested in a loser.

"To make matters worse, just around this time I ran into a general sales slump and needed some extra cash to replace an aging delivery truck. Since I used all of my reserve funds to buy the pencil sharpeners, there was nothing left for the truck. I had to turn to a bank and had to pay a 12 percent interest rate. I could have saved this interest charge if the cash I recklessly plowed into excess inventories was still in the bank."

Now you may think you have it all in perspective. The solution seems clear and simple: pare your inventories to the bone. Keep little or nothing in stock and buy only in response to customer orders. Sell off the warehouse; close up the back room; and eliminate the risk of unwanted merchandise.

The only problem is that you'll be eliminating most of your business as well. That is because inadequate inventories are just as dangerous as excess goods. The failure to have the right merchandise ready and waiting for customers when and where they want it means lost business. There's no two ways about it. If you do not have what it takes to fill the order, competitors will. You can bet on it.

So inventory management is, as we've said, a balance. A balance between market demand, future projections and your own cash resources. You must ask yourself: How much merchandise will I need on hand today? How much tomorrow? Is it likely that sales will suddenly drop off? Will sales suddenly pick up? How much cash can I allot for inventories?

As a rule of thumb, we recommend that you keep the following percentage of your average monthly sales in inventory:

*Hot-Selling Items: 45 percent
*Steady Movers: 30 percent
*Moderate Sellers: 20 percent
*Slow-Selling Items: 10 percent

Try these guidelines and see how they work for you. Feel free to make the changes necessary for your particular business. As long as you are testing, experimenting and evaluating inventory decisions, you are moving in the right direction. The idea is to bring science to inventory management. To turn inventory ignorance into inventory intelligence. Do this and you'll be way ahead of the crowd.

"Learning the mechanics of proper inventory controls saved me a lot of money—and a lot of headaches," Sarah adds. "After my episode with the pencil sharpeners, I was smart enough to apply some management techniques to my inventory function. Now I am rarely stuck with unwanted merchandise and I always have enough reserve cash to finance my own capital purchases. I save money both ways."

Maybe that's why Sarah employs 26 people, maintains four offices and runs a fleet of 12 trucks. She's a smart business-woman—and a rich one at that.

GETTING TOO BIG FOR YOUR BRITCHES:
How "super service" can turn on super sales

Look for the reasons companies fail and you're bound to turn up a list as long as your arm. Running a business is a complex affair: it's rare that a single reason can ever claim all the fault for a company's demise.

That's not to say that a small number of mistakes don't have an overwhelming impact on business failures. They do! Examine the histories of any group of bankrupt firms and you'll likely find a common thread of management errors running through them all. The essential point here is that while any commercial failure is due to a myriad problems, the cause of death can often be attributed to one of a few very common and devastating business mistakes.

Like "getting too big for your britches." What does that mean? Simply that too many small companies let a little success go to their heads. The owner-manager comes up with a winning idea, launches a business to sell it and quickly finds that customers flock to the firm in record numbers. Although this appears to be a scenario for success, it is, instead, the path to failure for thousands of firms.

Why? Because as soon as that first easy buck comes rolling in—as soon as that first crush of customers fills the store or factory—the inexperienced entrepreneur tends to forget all the basic lessons of professional business management. Most important, they forget that small companies must retain the "service factor" regardless of how big and successful the venture becomes. They forget that there must be a direct relationship between success and customer service. The bigger the company becomes the harder it must work to keep the service element strong.

The reason: today's loyal customer can be gone tomorrow—never to be seen again. Turn off even your best patrons with rude or inferior service and you've lost a friend to the competition. For no matter what you have to offer, chances are there will be strong competition around to match it. Don't be fooled into thinking that today's crowds will necessarily be there tomorrow. Just give them reason to turn away and the competition will do all the rest.

For a look at how the service factor can be kept strong regardless of the company's size, look at Sears. This largest of all the nation's retailers has soared in size over the years from a tiny merchandise outlet to a multi-billion dollar empire. Every major city in the nation boasts at least one Sears store and a healthy percentage of U.S. households order a wide variety of goods and services from the chain's catalogue. The company's slogan is true: Sears is "Where America Shops."

Why, in this nation of competing retailers, does Sears keep on expanding year after year while thousands of other would-be Sears fall by the wayside?

One reason for the company's success is clear: Sears has never abandoned its long-standing policy of providing excellent customer services. Success has never gone to Sears' head: the bigger the company has become the better its services.

Visit a Sears store. The proof is in the pudding. For the most part, Sears stores are spotlessly clean, well-staffed with trained and courteous clerks and the service is fast. All merchandise is guaranteed for quality, most catalog orders are delivered on time and credit is extended to all credit-worthy customers. In all, shopping at Sears has always remained a pleasant experience. Sears management has not lost sight of the fact that the total of the company's success is equal to the combined loyalty of its millions of individual customers.

It's a lesson that you, as a small business owner, must keep in mind every single day your doors are open to the public. Super customer services turn on big sales because it is the best way to attract new business and to keep the old. The company that keeps its base of established volume while continuously attracting incremental dollars is the company achieving extraordinary financial success.

Super customer services can help you do it. Here's how to establish a top-flight customer service program that can translate into big profits over the years:

1. Develop formal company standards for dealing with customers—put them in writing—and make sure that each and every employee complies.

2. Devise an established procedure for handling customer gripes. Make sure that all legitimate complaints receive a fair hearing from a responsible employee.

3. Make yourself available as the court of last resort for all customer complaints. Build in a safety valve in the complaint-handling system that automatically directs all stubborn problems to your attention. Customers always appreciate the boss' willingness to personally solve a sticky issue.

4. Initiate two customer service suggestion programs: one for use by employees and one by the customers themselves. The employee program can take the form of a suggestion box located in the back room, stock area or the like. Ask employees to drop in their ideas for improving the company's customer relations. To get them thinking, offer a $25 bond for every idea the company puts into practice. This can produce some excellent results: employees are often in tune with what customers want. Back this up with a customer generated feedback program. Along with every bill, invoice or promotional memo, include a form requesting the customer's opinions on the following questions:

>*Are sales personnel polite? Are they helpful
>   and well-informed?
>*Is one employee (by name) especially good or
>   bad to deal with?

*Are gripes handled to your satisfaction? If no,
    what are we doing wrong?
*How would you rate our customer service in
    general? What could be done to improve it?

5. Most important is to use these suggestion forms as living documents. That is, take firm and fast action to correct what customers perceive as deficiencies and to reward the kind of services they appreciate. If an employee gets frequent compliments from a number of customers, promote the individual or boost his compenstion. Popular employees are valuable assets. Treat them well.

6. Finally, appoint an intelligent and level-headed employee to supervise all customer relations on a daily basis. In small companies this need not be the individual's only assignment, but there should be one person with the authority and the knowledge to handle customers.

Taken together, these steps can go a long way towards preventing the loss of your most precious asset: loyal customers. They can go a long way towards building the kind of professionally-run company that avoids the common mistakes and keeps growing ever bigger and richer.

"Our customer-service suggestion program yielded an extra $10,000 in the first few months of its existence," explains Mel K., owner of an Arizona chain of dry cleaning outlets. "Since personal relationships with our good customers are so important in this business, I took up an employee's suggestion that we send out Christmas cards to every customer for whom we had an address.

"This simple courtesy, which I'd never thought of doing myself, produced a very favorable customer response. First of all, 285 customers returned the favor by sending us cards. And even more important, our post-Christmas business zoomed by more than $10,000. Not bad for a $25 investment in awarding the employee with a savings bond."

Not bad at all!

ADVERTISING TO THE WRONG PEOPLE:
How to select the right media
for your message

Solve this riddle. What management function do most small business owners think they know most about when in fact they know very little?

The answer is ADVERTISING. Few business functions yield nearly as much financial waste, aggravation and serious management mistakes as advertising. The reason is clear: in this most public of business activities, far too many owner-managers confuse familiarity with expertise. They are not the same.

Everyone is exposed to advertising: consumers and business owners alike get their daily doses of newspaper ads, radio jingles and television commercials. We all comment about advertising, react to it and alternately avoid it and act on it. We have our favorite campaigns—and the ones we hate with a passion. All in all, advertising is deeply ingrained in the American way of life.

And here is where the trouble lies. All of this exposure to advertising leads even the most inexperienced layman to develop strong opinions on what it takes to achieve advertising success. The newly-launched entrepreneur who knows enough to leave his company's tax returns to an accountant doesn't even hesitate to handle the entire advertising function without a single lesson in this surprisingly complex business science. When it comes to advertising, this "know it all" feeling leads millions of small business owner-managers to take that long, wasteful journey down the advertising wasteland. To pour scarce business funds into inefficient and unproductive business promotions. To sap the firm of its financial reserves and to deprive it of the genuine benefits professional advertising can deliver. It's a common mistake you can avoid.

Step one is to forget the glamor and the art of the campaign itself and think first of the all-important function of media selection. Where should the company's ads appear? The choices are endless: radio, TV, billboards, direct mail, circulars, newspapers, magazines. . . . Since this crucial decision determines the audience you'll reach, it's a vital first step to successful advertising—yet it is a step most inexperienced owner-managers overlook.

Use Chart 1 to review some of the comparative features of available media.

The terms in the chart refer to the various techniques used for evaluating media. For example, "cost effectiveness" refers to the amount of business likely to be generated by the advertising investment. A very effective medium has a very good rating: volume generated far exceeds the amount of the advertising investment.

The "required investment level" is the term for the amount of financial investment required to produce an effective small business campaign in the particular medium. This measurement includes expenses for the medium itself (radio time, magazine space, etc.) as well as associated production costs (commercial film, photography, agency fees, etc.).

The ratings in the media selection chart are broad generalizations and are meant only as a guide for your initial planning. Although local television, for example, is listed as only fairly-cost effective, this medium can, if used for the right campaign, produce volume exceeding 100 times the advertising investment.

So use the chart as a general guideline but feel free to experiment on your own. In all business activities, trial and error helps management achieve the ideal approach. See what works best for your company—and stick with it.

The idea is to start off with as much basic information as you

CHART 1

MEDIA	COST-EFFECTIVE RATING	REQUIRED INVESTMENT LEVEL	BEST USE	TYPICAL RESPONSE
NEWSPAPER	Good	Modest	Regular campaign stressing price & product information	Excellent traffic builder—
LOCAL TELEVISION	Fair to good	Can be high (production costs)	Special sales covering broad market area	Big turnout but not all serious buyers
LOCAL RADIO	Good	Fairly high	Reaching specific market groups (teenage stations, etc.)	Very good if specific offer is made
LOCAL MAGAZINE	Fair to good	Modest	For relating technical information	Depends heavily on quality of the ad
BILLBOARD	Fair to poor	Substantial	Image-building & special promotions (grand opening, etc.)	High awareness
DIRECT MAIL	Fair to good	High to modest	Reaching isolated groups (doctors)	Very small percentage of total market

can muster. The more you know the less likely you are to pour thousands of dollars down the drain in poorly-planned and unproductive advertising sprees. The media selection chart can help you get started on the right foot. So too can Chart 2, the "Media by Business Type Selector."

CHART 2

MEDIUM	RETAIL BUSINESS	WHOLE-SALE BUSINESS	TECHNICAL COMPANY	MANUFAC-TURER	PRICE-ORIENTED FIRM	IMAGE-ORIENTED FIRM
LOCAL TV	×					×
LOCAL RADIO	×	×				×
NEWSPAPER	×				×	×
MAGAZINE	×	×	×	×		×
BILLBOARD	×					×
DIRECT MAIL	×	×	×	·×	×	

Using this chart is simple. Just identify your type of business and look down the column for the kinds of media recommended for it. Bear in mind again, however, that these are generalizations—meant to give you a starting point for developing your own media strategy.

"Using media selection guides can really help you reach customers where their wallets are," says Dinah L., an independent cosmetics manufacturer from Savannah, Georgia. "When I first started out in this business I made the common mistake of thinking that TV advertising is the only game in town—the best medium for every type of promotion.

"I was dead wrong—and I wasted $41,000 in the process. The problem was, my TV ads were costly and yet were reaching thousands of people like men, children and senior citizens who had no interest in my cosmetics."

Dinah's strategy took an abrupt about face when she spotted her first media selection chart in a business magazine. She put a halt to all TV ads and put her money instead into a fashionable and trendy magazine appealing to Savannah's young and affluent women.

"Suddenly," she adds, "sales soared through the clouds. The high-quality magazine photography added to my products' image—and add this to the fact that we were now reaching all prime sales prospects—well, now you know why I've become a magazine fanatic. I've been able to cut my ad budget to $55,000 per year while simultaneously boosting sales 270 percent. That's what I call success."

We do too. Congratulations Dinah!

ADVERTISING WITHOUT ORIGINALITY: How hot-shot campaigns can put your company on the map

It's no secret that there's more to profitable advertising than simply selecting the right media. Important as this is, it is only the first step. The big gun—the design of the actual ads—must command the highest level of time, effort, talent and money.

Again—most small business owners trip up here. In the mad rush to apply what little knowledge they have of successful advertising, millions of entrepreneurs commit the identical error: the use of tired old cliches which attract only a smidgen of attention, interest few and do little to put their companies on the commercial map.

As in the case of haphazard media selection, poor advertising development is usually due to that "know it all" syndrome. Constant exposure to popular advertising techniques leads many owner-managers to believe that these are the only strategies that work.

"Let's take the example of using a humorous type of spokesman in TV ads," explains Jan D., president of a suburban New York advertising agency. "A lot of inexperienced business owners see this approach used time and again and think that it must automatically work for every kind of product and service. So as soon as they start advertising their own business, they hire a clown or a half-baked comedian, come up with some foolish jokes, and think all the consumers in the area are going to come rushing in. In reality, all they get is a lot of media and production bills and very little, if any, increase in sales volume. It's a costly business mistake.

"The problem is that while a funny skit may generate sales for a new brand of children's cereal, it doesn't work for a local department store. When judging department stores, people want to know what kind of merchandise is sold; what the prices are; and what kind of service they can expect. The advertising must touch on these features."

The idea, then, is to come up with fresh and dramatic approaches to your specific advertising objectives. To abandon the tired cliches and to cut through the so-called clutter of competing ads with dynamic communications that *Sell*.

Experts in print, broadcast and related media recommend the following guidelines to designing hot-shot small budget ad campaigns that can put your company on the map:

*Strive for groundbreaking concepts and strategies. A west coast used car dealer, for example, hit pay dirt by starring in his own local TV ads smashing up a car with an axe. The approach was so unique that it garnered an extraordinary amount of attention—and the dealer's sales soared as a result.

*Whether you are promoting a product, service or a store, build your advertising around the USP—The Unique Selling Point. This refers to the one feature or characteristic which distinguishes your offering from that of the competition. The USP for Cadillac cars, for example, is luxury size and elegance. This, therefore, is the main element of the company's advertising.

In today's highly-competitive markets, the USP is more crucial than ever. Increasingly sophisticated consumers must have a genuine reason for purchasing your item over the competition's.

*Once you have determined the USP, drive the point home to all potential customers through use of "positioning." This marketing technique refers to the establishment of the USP in the public's mind. Think of the "one beer to have when you're having more than one" and most of us automatically think of Schaefer beer. That's because for years the beer has been "positioned" as the brand for those who drink a lot of beer.

Positioning makes us equate heavy beer drinking with Schaefer—just the association the company wants.

Consistency, above all else, is the secret to effective positioning. To establish the USP—to properly position the product or service—you must hit home on the same theme time and again, year after year. Don't make the common mistake of inexperienced advertisers: don't change your advertising approach with every change in the weather. Develop a winner and stay with it. Look at Marlboro cigarettes, for example. In this classic case of successful positioning, the company's cowboy image has been the hottest thing in the cigarette industry for years. As long as it keeps working, Marlboro has no intention of changing its ad theme. Why should it? The cowboy has made Marlboro the leading brand in the nation.

*Follow up on all advertising ventures with a formal program of testing and evaluation. Did the ad boost sales? Did it enhance the company's image? Did your approach put people off rather than turning them on?

These are among the questions you'll want to answer before continuing to spend money on your ad campaign. You need feedback. Feedback to help you redesign ads, change your approach, select new media or increase your spending. The more you know about how your advertising is working, the better equipped you'll be to make it more effective. A savvy owner-manager recognizes that there is endless opportunity to fine-tune ads to generate ever-greater consumer response.

The required feedback is available from a number of sources. Make random telephone calls to local consumers; slip a brief questionnaire in your monthly billing; talk with customers at your place of business and ask employees. This wide diversity of opinions will help you come up with that "hot shot" campaign you know is possible.

To show just how phenomenally successful small business advertising can be, let's look at the now classic case of New York's JGE appliances. By initiating a bold, new type of TV campaign, the owner-manager of a sleepy appliance store turned his business into a roaring retail giant.

Rather than relying on the tired cliche of a slick announcer, JGE ads featured the owner himself dressed in old pants, a Tshirt and a hard hat. The no-frills, no-nonsense approach appealed to the city's blue collar workers—appealed in a way no traditional advertising had ever done before.

The morning after the first ads ran, JGE was swamped with lines of eager consumers fighting to get in the doors. And that was only the beginning: in no time at all the meager little retail shop grew into one of New York's largest retail empires, grossing more than $80 million per year.

Proof positive of the power of inventive thinking—the power of well-planned small business advertising.

PROMOTIONAL OVERKILL:
How to prevent diminishing returns on your business promotions

Now that we have isolated successful strategies for advertising promotions, we are left to deal with a final question—and it is perhaps the biggest question of all. How much do we spend to make the advertising work? How much money do we invest to make the promotion succeed?

One thing is for sure: we can not simply pull a number out of thin air. Guessing at the proper level of promotional spending is not only unprofessional—it is also a very risky way to run a business. And yet it is one of the most common of all business mistakes: most small business owner-managers either spend far too much or too little on advertising budgets.

Surprisingly, those entrepreneurs with some knowledge of advertising tend towards the former: they overspend by up to 200 to 400 percent more than is required to conduct effective ad campaigns. The reason: having devised a winning strategy (the ideal combination of media and message), these owner-managers believe that the more money they pour into this strategy the more profits they will reap.

A closer look at this reasoning reveals its basic fallacy. First, small companies can not afford unlimited advertising expenditures. Cash, in our capital-scarce economy, is a rare commodity required for other than promotional needs. For a small business to grow, it must also set aside funds for capital equipment, larger facilities and research. Every available dollar can not be thrown into an open-ended ad campaign.

But even more important, over-inflated advertising budgets collide with a basic law of mathematics: the law of diminishing returns. Stated technically, this is "the rate of yield that beyond a certain point fails to increase in proportion to additional investments."

Put simply, this means that in any spending program there comes a point at which additional investments can not be justified in terms of additional sales. That's the law of diminishing returns.

Here's how it works in real life. When Andy K. of San Francisco, California quit his job with a leading west coast bread and cake distributor, he did so for a purpose. After years of planning successful new products for the corporation, Andy wanted to use his talents to amass personal wealth.

His idea: to sell the first packaged cookies that could be warmed without over-cooking in a regular household toaster. Since everyone likes the taste of hot cookies—but few want to bother baking them—Andy's idea looked like a winner. And his advertising strategy proved just the thing to get the new product, called "HOT COOKIES," off the ground.

Finding that local magazines would be the ideal medium for his message, Andy bought full-page ads in a number of leading journals. The ad concept was simple and unique: the bold headline stated HOT COOKIES; simple copy explained the product; and at the bottom readers were invited to scratch the page for a sample aroma of how the new cookies smell when warmed in the toaster. (An increasingly popular process enables advertisers to capture specific aromas for print ads.)

After only two weeks of advertising, there was no question that Andy's new product would go straight to the top. Retailers were literally besieged with advance orders and thousands of eager consumers called Andy directly. The rush was on: in three months Andy signed on five major supermarket chains and 536 independent grocers. Sales were $36,000 per month with advertising expenses weighing in at about $7000 per month.

Thinking that more advertising would push sales even higher, Andy stepped up spending to $10,000 per month by adding two more magazines to the media schedule. And sure enough, sales soared even higher, reaching $86,500 per month after the first full year of sales.

That's when Andy let success go to his head and started making the common mistake of overspending. Believing there was no end to HOT COOKIES sale increases, Andy doubled the ad budget to $20,000 per month, mostly by taking two full page ads in each of the scheduled magazines. That's an additional expense of $120,000 per year—a significant sum for a small firm, and as it turned out, a major waste for Andy's company.

By the time he got around to measuring sales, Andy discovered that the doubling in advertising expenditures hardly budged his monthly volume. From January to June the extra $10,000 per month in ad fees produced only $3,000 per month in extra sales. That's a $42,000 loss—the extra advertising was not generating high enough incremental sales. Andy had reached the point of diminishing returns. It was time to cut back the budget to the $10,000 per month level.

Lucky for Andy, he discovered his overspending before the losses could build up to really dangerous levels. Many other owner-managers are not as fortunate: inflated ad budgets have been known to waste as much as a few million dollars a year—millions of dollars the companies could have put into productive growth ventures.

How can owner-managers avoid the problem of diminishing returns? How can you protect against inflated advertising budgets? How can management determine the ideal investment in productive advertising?

Although there are no simple answers, the best approach is to develop a formal budget for promotional spending. As with all such projects, it is a good idea to prepare a special notebook for this purpose, using it to jot down all relevant facts, figures and mathematical formulas. The following points are meant as a general guideline for preparing a promotional budget:

1. The promotion budget should be based on a percentage of actual or projected sales. This percentage varies depending on the type of product or service involved:

Consumer-oriented package goods—
  six to twelve percent
Big ticket consumer goods—
  four to eight percent
Consumer services—
  five to eight percent
Industrial equipment—
  two to four percent

2. In general, spending for new products should be at the higher end of the scale. For example, an established packaged good item like bath soap may require only a six percent of sales ad budget while a brand new type of cake mix may need a twelve percent budget to build maximum sales.

3. Promotional budgeting should be done on a yearly basis with reviews of all sales and spending figures performed quarterly. This review procedure gives managers the opportunity to spot potential diminishing returns situations and to adjust spending accordingly.

4. If sales statistics warrant, push the advertising budget beyond the allocated levels—but do so gradually. Never be afraid to feed the budget if incremental investments are more than compensated for by additional revenues. Leave a 10 percent margin for expansion in every month's budget level.

As with all business plans, use personal experience and other expert advice to round out your promotional budgets. Help in this area is available from newspaper and magazine sales representatives. In addition, numerous advertising reports and studies are available by writing the Newspaper Advertising Bureau, 485 Lexington Ave., N.Y.C.

So gather all the information you can, prepare an initial promotion budget, check this against your actual experience in the marketplace and then adjust the budget accordingly. Use trial and error, research and good hard data and you'll likely come up with the ideal promotion budget for your business. A budget geared to attain the highest possible sales at the lowest possible cost.

GETTING LOST AMONG THE COMPETITION:
How a little "show biz" can make your firm a household name

Have you ever noticed how some companies shine like the northern star, while others are mired in hopeless obscurity? How some company names become household words, while others are never even noticed? It's no accident. That some companies stand out from the pack—grab all the attention, publicity and dollars— is no accident at all. It is purely the result of wise management working behind the scenes—of savvy business owners who know what it takes to command the public's attention.

When it comes down to the bottom line, it takes a little show biz. It takes a little razzle-dazzle business showmanship to move a company from the chorus line to center stage. Call it advertising, publicity or merchandising, the essential thing is that you woo your market to come your way.

The idea is to avoid the common mistake of getting lost in the crowd. To use showmanship to stand out from the thousands of competitors all across the nation selling the same things in the same way that you do. All too many small business owners think there is no room in the business world for personal inventiveness. Just the opposite is true. The really original entrepreneur—the one who does things differently and avoids the beaten path—is most often the one the public remembers. More important, he is the one the public patronizes.

One of the best opportunities to be original is in the function of merchandising. This crucial function, which is often ignored in small business, encompasses everything a company does to display and present attractive products or services to its buying public. When you get down to it, merchandising is really a fancy word for selling.

How can you be original when it comes to selling? Easy! Rather than simply doing things the way everyone else does, or the way tradition demands they be done, why not let your mind roam free and try to think of new and better ways of selling. Try to be an inventive merchandiser. Success at this can make your firm a household name.

Let's see how this has worked successfully on a larger scale. Take the case of Bloomingdale's department stores. When you talk about Bloomingdale's, you are talking about one of the great business success stories of all times.

"Bloomies," as the store is affectionately known by its millions of customers, is in a class by itself. Consumers do more than shop at the store in record numbers—they also love it. That's right! They actually love the store. Love to visit it, stroll the aisles, eat in the restaurants, meet their friends there and, most important, shop, shop, shop.

It wasn't always this way. Bloomingdale's started out like any other store selling a wide variety of goods to Manhattan-based New Yorkers. But then, after many years of business, Bloomingdale's found itself operating in a unique neighborhood —the so-called Gold Coast of Manhattan's East Side. Here New York's wealthy upper crust lives and shops—and Bloomies decided to cater to this market. How? By launching bold new directions in retail merchandising.

Bloomingdale's put itself on the map as the number one store by being the first to treat shopping as an "experience" rather than a chore. Enter Bloomingdale's and you notice this from the start: like an old-world bazaar, exotic and colorful merchandise is displayed so that customers can touch, smell and handle the goods.

The best way to describe Bloomingdale's is as a "living" store. Everything the firm sells comes to life—and it's all planned that way. For example, to capitalize on the new-found popularity of clothes, furniture and artifacts from the People's Republic of China, Bloomindale's enveloped its entire store in a Chinese motif. Displays were dressed with bamboo umbrellas, Chinese lanterns lit the aisles and a Chinese chef actually prepared delicacies to be tasted by customers right on the main selling floors.

These "theme" promotions—which distinguish Bloomingdale's from its lesser competitors—are fine examples of fresh and original merchandising. The kind of merchandising you can duplicate to make a name for your firm—and to chalk up hefty sales in the process.

Inventive merchandising then, can help you avoid the common mistake of getting lost in the competitive shuffle. It can help you achieve the kind of flat-out success that turns small businesses into money machines.

Here are four suggestions for *Merchandising Magic:*

1. Plan a regular series of company-wide promotional themes. Let the theme run through all aspects of your operations— merchandise selection, displays and advertising.

Let's say, for example, that you hold an annual autumn promotion. To distinguish your fall promotion from everyone else's, do something bold and original. Like distribute sales circulars to your best customers with an apple tucked inside. Or set up an apple cider stand right outside your shop and offer free samples to all passersby. Maybe even hold an apple dunking contest and give away free merchandise to the winner.

Best of all, hold all of these promotions simultaneously and feature each and every one in your advertising. You'll produce that sense of excitement so crucial to successful merchandising and you may even get some valuable free publicity from the local newspaper, TV or radio station.

2. More on the subject of publicity: strive for so-called "media events." These are the extravagant business promotions of such

unusual interest that the local media comes out in force to cover the event. The benefit to you is clear: you get top notch publicity free of charge—the kind of dramatic publicity you could not duplicate with paid advertising.

Take the case of a well-known restauranteur in New York City. When he decided to open his newest eating establishment in Manhattan's famed Central Park, the owner staged a full-fledged media event. He built the largest ice cream sundae ever made—several feet high and wide—and invited the public to eat it for free.

The stunt paid off handsomely. Even in New York—which is a tough nut to crack for publicity—the event was featured on the evening TV news and in major newspapers. The restaurant, which has since become an all-out success, was on the map the very first day its doors opened. That's what you call getting a leg up on the competition.

3. Try to take the lead in merchandise selection. This means trying to anticipate public tastes far before a widespread fad has developed. This will earn your firm a reputation as an innovator and will enable you to grab off the lion's share of the market before the competition knows what hit it.

Another New York-based store, Hamacher Shlemmer, has achieved great success over many years by taking this very role of merchandise innovator. The store's management shops the world for unique products and is usually way ahead of everyone else in starting national trends. Hamacher Shlemmer, for example, was the first store to sell the Mr. Coffee machine—one of the most successful products ever introduced in the U.S. So for some time, Hamacher had the market for this extremely popular product all to itself. That's what you call reaping the benefits of heads-up merchandising.

Finding trend-setting merchandise is not as hard as you may think. All you really have to do is look for it. Try travelling to those foreign countries that are off the beaten path (nations in Indochina, Latin America, etc.). You'll likely find strange and attractive locally produced goods. Or put out the call to inventors and designers of unusual merchandise and you'll get thousands of exotic items to consider.

4. Finally, just sit down and *think*. *Think* of some way that you can do something different and original—something that will put your company on the map. It does not have to be costly or extravagant: just novel and attention-getting. Suppose all your competitors are open for business from nine to five, be the first to stay open till midnight. Just a simple act like this will help build your reputation as an innovator—and you'll likely profit from it. Another idea: hire an avant-garde window trimmer to do something outlandish with your display windows. One store in Chicago put a live cow in the window as part of a display and thousands turned out to witness the event. Those who did never forgot that store—never!

Now it's your turn. Start thinking up new ways to make your company a local celebrity.

UNDERINSURING YOUR COMPANY: How to be sure your business will go on despite sudden tragedy

Of all the tragic business mistakes, perhaps the most important is the failure to purchase sufficient insurance. Lack of adequate coverage can wipe you out before you know what hit you.

Problem is, too many small business owners look at insurance, of all things, as a way to cut corners. They fail to recognize that operating without insurance is not economizing—it's gambling. Putting hard-earned investments into an underinsured business is like building a house of cards: one sudden setback and the roof caves in.

The biggest mistake is to set an arbitrary limit on insurance spending. That's pure nonsense. The only way to compute your maximum spending is to determine your maximum vulnerability. For every major risk you must have compensating coverage. It is absolutely essential. After all, you are in business for the long run not for days, weeks or until the first disaster strikes.

Insurance is a crucial aspect of your total business operation. So take all the time you need to study your coverage requirements. In addition to standard, run-of-the-mill policies, modern business insurance can protect you in a number of little-known ways.

All you have to do is explore the options. Typical of all too many entrepreneurs, Harvey K. of Kansas City, Kansas never bothered to do just that. So as his highly-profitable laundry service grew to be the largest in town, he retained the same basic fire and theft protection he'd purchased in the first year of operation. This was a source of pride—and he boasted quite often of his low annual premiums.

It turned out to be false pride. Two weeks after closing out a very successful year, Harvey's boasting came to a screeching halt. The reason: he faced the worst setback of his business career—a sudden and unexpected jolt.

The giant Futura Hotel—Harvey's biggest commercial customer, alone responsible for 75 percent of his revenues—was swept by fire on a cold and windy January morning. In less than five hours, huge sections of the inn were gutted, the interior completely destroyed by fire. The prognosis: rebuilding would take three to five months. For the time being, the Futura would close its doors, accepting no guests and requiring no laundry services.

For Harvey, the fire proved to be a personal financial disaster. Deprived of a substantial chunk of revenues for up to six months, the laundry was forced into bankruptcy. There was simply not enough cash coming in to pay salaries, rent, utilities and the myriad other expenses of a large and growing business.

The sad truth is that the bankruptcy was completely unnecessary. The hardship, the hand wringing and the eventual insolvency—all could have been easily avoided. How? Simply by purchasing an obscure form of business insurance readily available to anyone who knows enough to ask for it. Known as "Business Interruption Insurance," the coverage protects you against loss of income due to the temporary shut down of your business or that of a major customer.

Business Interruption Insurance is designed to carry you through the toughest business crisis—to keep income flowing so that the firm can stay afloat in spite of sudden disasters. Most policies cover continuing expenses, reimbursing most costs required to maintain normal business operations.

Another obscure, yet equally-rewarding form of business insurance is "Key Man Protection." This policy insures your firm against the death of a valued partner or executive.

Let's say you own a sales-oriented business and your top man brings in $400,000 a year in contracts. He does it all on longtime personal contacts, and so he's hard as hell to replace.

The best bet here is to purchase Key Man Protection on the executive's life. In the event of his death, the company will be paid a large enough lump sum to compensate for declining sales until a new man or woman can be trained to replace the deceased.

Finally, there's Bad Debt Insurance. Credit losses cost the nation's businesses $3 billion annually—and the toll is rising. High bankruptcy rates and poor payment practices are forcing more and more companies to write off bad debts at substantial losses.

Managers can, however, reduce the likelihood of substantial losses by tightening up credit standards and by buying bad debt insurance. This little-known type of insurance coverage offers financial protection against sudden losses due to customer bankruptcies.

Commercial credit coverage (bad debt) is a form of "excess loss insurance." It is a guarantee to manufacturers, jobbers, wholesalers and service companies that they will be reimbursed for bad debts sustained in excess of a specified deductible. That's the beauty of bad debt insurance: it limits your loss exposure.

All business insurance shares a single, overriding objective—the elimination of unnecessary risk. Building a profitable commercial venture is tough enough without the complicating factor of uninsured disasters. There is no reason at all to invest your time and effort in a business just to see it all go up in smoke.

You can control business risks. You must! Talk over the alternatives with a qualified business insurance broker. You may be lacking any one of a number of policies just right for your business.

NEGLECTING THE TAX AUDIT:
How to use tax guidelines for your benefit

THE TAX AUDIT—few things strike more fear in the hearts of business owners. Why? Fear of the unexpected, for one. Although we all know that tax audits are grueling grill sessions with the IRS—unpleasant experiences to say the least—we rarely know what the tax man has up his sleeve. And that's what worries us.

No more! It is no longer excusable to go to a tax audit unprepared. That's because there is now a way to break the shroud of secrecy around the audit procedure. Revealing information on small business tax audits is now available to the public under provisions of the Freedom of Information Act. The act has forced the Internal Revenue Service (IRS) to release business audit manuals for public review. For the first time, you can learn in advance what to expect from IRS audits. By reviewing IRS guidelines, managers can become familiar with IRS procedures, key areas of inquiry and types of recognized supporting documents. What better way to walk in well prepared?

Gaining access to the once-secret guidelines is quite simple. IRS district offices in most large cities now have special reading rooms reserved solely for the public inspection of audit manuals.

Entrepreneurs interested in specific documents need simply inform the clerk and the manuals will be brought to you. Duplication services are also available for a small fee based on the number of pages copied.

You are entitled to review IRS audit manuals covering individual and partnership tax returns, collection division manuals, appellate division manuals and other documents pertaining to a wide range of IRS operations. Audit manuals, which are most important to businessmen, are prepared by the IRS for agents making field examinations of income tax returns. Agents use the manuals as standard guides for handling audited returns.

The following are examples of key audit procedures for individual business and partnership returns. You are advised to visit IRS offices for a thorough review of all applicable standards. If called for an audit, you are also advised to seek legal and financial assistance.

*Agents will review with management any unusual events occurring during the period under examination. It is a good idea, in light of this, to carefully document exceptional losses, unusually high costs and other factors which might be considered extraordinary.

*Close attention is paid to the lines of executive authority. Agents want to know who is authorized to make accounting decisions and who can approve cash payments to officers.

*In the event of an audit, agents are likely to ask you for business ledgers, journals, accountants' reports, procedural manuals and related financial documents. Keeping your books neat, orderly and accurate is the best way to be prepared.

*Agents will want to know how you computed gains or losses on the sale of assets. Be prepared to provide detailed information on the holding period, expense of sale, selling price and other contributing factors.

*IRS guidelines suggest close scrutiny of all deductions for bad debts. Agents will want a full list of accounts charged off, including names, dates and dollar amounts.

*Incomplete business records are likely to trigger IRS

audits. If so, agents may trace your bank accounts, real estate holdings and living expenses to secure the desired information. You are advised to work with lawyers and accountants throughout the investigation.

Arnold B. knew enough to devote a full week to preparing for his encounter with the tax collector. And it turned out to be time well spent.

When asked about a questionable loss on the sale of an abandoned furniture warehouse, Arnold had just the legal ammunition he needed to prove the deduction. A detailed ledger spelled out the exact holding period, all related selling expenses (including promotional services) and notarized verification of the selling price.

The happy ending should come as no surprise. Arnold won his case hands down—the declared deductions remained intact. And as Arnold's attorney noted as they left the audit hearing room, "Your work in preparing for this audit just saved you $10,000. So buy me lunch—you can afford it."

UNPROFITABLE PRICING:
How to "build in" hefty profits

Believe it or not, the simplest of all business procedures, setting prices, is a total mystery to the vast majority of business owners. Most never give it a thought; others think they know it all without bothering to examine whether they really do. In either case, substantial losses often result. It is simply an inexcusable mistake to set arbitrary or standard prices, for in most cases these turn out to be unprofitable prices.

Let's get down to brass tacks. As an independent entrepreneur you bring products or services to market in return for specified fees. These fees are your compensation—your business income. You want to make sure to earn a lucrative profit for your efforts.

The question is, how do you determine if the fees you charge are adequate for the products or services rendered? How do you know you are being sufficiently reimbursed to earn a hefty business profit? How do you know you are charging enough to cover costs, risks and personal expenses?

The answer to all of the above is intelligent pricing. You must adopt a systematic approach to establishing prices: an approach that assures you of consistent profits after all costs are accounted and paid. Your goal, then, is to compute a balanced markup percentage, one high enough to be profitable and to make you and your business financially healthy.

The determination of markup percentages can never be left to habit or instinct—to do so is a mistake. Yet many entrepreneurs set prices according to personal intuition; others rely instead on manufacturers' suggestions. Both are often wrong: pricing is too important to base on whims or generalizations.

Determining the ideal markup for your products and services is your responsibility. To do so, you'll want to consider the actual costs you incur in providing business products or services—the amount of investment you will have to make over the years—and the level of cash profits required to make you financially comfortable and economically independent.

By considering all these factors, you will be sure to avoid unprofitable pricing. Remember at all times that you want to consider the best way to achieve maximum profits—and pricing can have a major impact on this. Your choice is to seek either a relatively high markup on a small sales volume or you can boost the volume by reducing the markup.

If your small venture suddenly grows into a formidable enterprise, the time may come to reduce the markup in order to attract even more customers. When to take this step, and how far you can go, can be figured through a process called "equating velocities," which works as follows: let's say your business is operating on a 33 percent gross margin and you want to reduce this to 30 percent in order to draw customers from the competition. Before taking this step, you must determine the amount of increased sales volume you'll need to yield—in dollars—a gross margin at least as large as the margin you now earn.

To get the answer, divide the present markup by the lower figure under consideration: in this case, 33 percent divided by 30 = 1.10. So for every dollar of your present volume, 1.10 or 10 percent more in sales will be needed to compensate for the lower markup. If you are relatively sure the lower markup will boost sales considerably more than 10 percent, then the cut in markup may be a good business move. Just think, sales may soar by 50 percent or more—making you the richer for it.

Now you know how to gauge your markup scientifically. How to avoid unprofitable pricing and assure yourself of lucrative financial rewards.

LEANING ON LADY LUCK:
How business counseling can turn the odds in your favor

*I. Every business venture is,
to some extent, a gamble.*

*II. Basing business management
on gambler's luck is the best way
to drive a company into swift
and irreversible bankruptcy.*

At first glance, these two statements may seem contradictory: if one is right, the other must be wrong. This initial impression, however, is not true. Take a closer look and you'll see that both statements are correct. What do we mean by this? First, that starting and running any kind of business does involve a gamble. In business, there is no such animal as a sure thing. For every venture the owners thought would succeed and did, there is an Edsel that went just the other way. So whenever an entrepreneur designs a product, opens a store or launches a new service there is always a chance that the time and money invested will go right down the drain. It's a gamble.

But that is only half the story. Once we realize that there are risks involved in starting a business, that, for the most part, is where the gambling should end. Once you are established you may, of course, want to take a long shot on a hot new product, location or other opportunity. But for all intents and purposes, the business must be run as a professionally-managed venture. That is the only way to build a sound and prosperous company.

You simply can not run a business the same way that you go to the race track—win one day and lose another. You are not looking for the fast buck here: your goal is to establish a longstanding enterprise that will grow more prosperous and stable with the years. Leaning on lady luck will not get you the prize you are after. Although your luck may hold out for awhile, you are bound to be a loser in the end.

In business, the winners are those who avoid the temptation to take the easy way out—those who avoid the temptation to rely on luck rather than sound business management almost always wind up ahead in the end. The great commercial successes from IBM to General Motors were built on hard work and solid business management—not on a roll of the dice.

What it all boils down to is this: as a business owner-manager your days will be filled with decisions: how much to invest; when to order; who to hire and promote; when to borrow; where to borrow; when to expand.

You can make these decisions based on two foundations: shot-in-the-dark guesses or proven business principles. The latter, although it may take more time, effort and research, is almost always the better way to go. Better by far.

The next logical question is how do you obtain the know-how and the expertise required to make educated business decisions? How do you get the kind of hard business data you can substitute for lady luck?

Well, first things first. Whether you are a seasoned entrepreneur or are just getting your feet wet with a spanking new business, you can not be expected to have expertise in all the complex facets of modern business management. Nor do you have the time to learn it all! So what do you do? Simple. You turn to the thousands of business consultants all across the nation who are specially trained to help you solve your business problems.

There has never been a better time to use consultants to improve the efficiency—and more important the profitability—of your business. That's because in this age of specialization, there are consultants ready and willing to help you with everything from finance to advertising, from manufacturing to insurance. All you have to do is locate the experts best suited to help your firm and then use their knowledge to help you deal with the uncertainties of business ownership. That is the only way to face the inevitable risks with the odds in your favor.

The following is a list of the major consulting services available to you. Why not jot down the names and addresses in a notebook reserved solely for memos concerning consulting services.

*The Small Business Administration (SBA) is the leading government-supported source for small business consulting services. SBA experts provide a wide range of counseling services and are especially adept at helping novice entrepreneurs get new businesses off the ground. In addition, the SBA publishes a comprehensive series of books and pamphlets on virtually every aspect of business management. Most of the publications are free; others are available for a slight charge.

SBA services are available to business owners through a network of district offices located in communities throughout the U.S. Here you can work with counseling experts and can obtain order forms for SBA publications. Check the white pages of your telephone book under U.S. Government listing for the address of your nearest SBA office or write to the SBA at Small Business Administration, Washington, D.C. 20416.

*To many business owners, consulting services offered by The Service Corps of Retired Executives (SCORE) will be highly attractive. The key benefit here is that SCORE counselors are former business owners and executives—they have practical experience facing the challenges and hurdles you are facing now. This real-world experience can be extremely valuable to entrepreneurs seeking expert advice.

SCORE services are part of the Small Business Administration and like the SBA, there is no charge for counseling. Check for the nearest SCORE office under SBA telephone listings or write directly to the SBA.

*Private consultants can be found in most major cities, with the greatest concentration of these firms located in the big metropolitan areas. Consulting firms run the full gamut from small, one-man shops to huge firms housing 100 or more experts. Some firms concentrate on a single specialty; others will tackle virtually every aspect of business management. Fees are also quite varied, running anywhere from $100 to $1,000 a day.

Although consulting outfits are listed in the yellow pages of your telephone book, it is not a good idea to just pick out the names at random. You will want to find a competent and reputable firm—and one with some experience in your field of business. So try talking with business associates, trade groups and the like before making a selection.

*Colleges and universities are one of the great untapped sources of business counseling. Many colleges consider it a public service to the community to offer the services of business students and professors. By making contacts here, you'll benefit from the very latest developments in business science and you'll get it all for little or no cost (depending on the college). Here again you may want to contact the SBA for a list of colleges this agency is funding to provide small business counseling services. (Ask for information on the Small Business Institute Program.)

*Valuable counseling services are also available from a number of other sources such as trade associations, banks, chambers of commerce and insurance companies. It is good practice to check out all of the opportunities available to you.

"The important thing is to eliminate as much of the guesswork as possible," says Arlen K., owner of an immensely successful dry cleaning chain in Los Angeles.

"I simply can not stress it enough how important this can be. Take my experience, for example. With the popularity of all the new miracle and permanent press fabrics, a lot of garments that used to go to the cleaners are now being cleaned at home. I started to see the evidence of this from continuous declines in my sales volume. People were clearly using the dry cleaners less and less.

"I really didn't know how to overcome the problem so I just

gambled and decided to open up two more stores, figuring that this would give me greater access to whatever market there was for dry cleaning. To make a long story short, my gamble rolled snake eyes and I wound up with the same deteriorating sales volume but now with steeply higher costs."

Only the very real threat of bankruptcy brought Arlen to where he should have gone in the first place: to the local SCORE office. There counselor Dwight J, a retired retail merchant himself, put Arlen's cleaning business back on the road to profitability.

Dwight's strategy: to sell off the two newest stores and to close down the three older units suffering the most dramatic sales declines. This prompt action saved $72,000 per month in operating expenses—more than enough to put the chain back into the black.

The next step was to invest a portion of these savings into a massive advertising and merchandising campaign designed to counter the trend towards home garment cleaning. Flyers, circulars and newspaper ads spelled out the danger of ruining delicate garments by using home cleaning agents and other non-professional techniques. Other promotions stressed the superior reputation of Arlen's stores and offered special discount cards for new customers.

"SCORE's strategy gave my business just the shot-in-the-arm it needed," Arlen explains. "We cut out our losing units that were draining the chain and we countered the movement away from dry cleaning. This one-two punch boosted sales by $1.1 million per year. That's reason enough to use counseling rather than gambling."

THINKING TOO "SMALL": How to capture your share of the really rich markets

Simple as it may sound, many small companies stay small because their owners never dare to think big. It's true: negative or defeatist thinking is the greatest obstacle to business success. As long as the entrepreneur thinks of himself as a nickle and dime operator, his company will never be more than a financial midget scratching around for subsistence earnings.

It is an easy trap to fall victim to. You do, after all, run a small venture with relatively few employees and limited capital. You know you can not compete head on with the likes of IBM or Sears—you would not stand a prayer. So you accept your role as second-class citizen and go off scrounging for dollars in the small markets the big boys don't want to bother with. You search for the crumbs they leave behind.

Accepting this role is an inexcusable business mistake. It is like drawing a circle around your company and promising not to grow any bigger than these artificial borders. There is no longer any need to accept this kind of obstacle.

Although it is true that you can not compete head on with the giants of industry, you can go after some of the lush, lucrative markets they have been reaping for years. You can do so by carving out a segment of these markets open to small business competitors.

All you really have to do is change your way of thinking. Set your sights on the big apple. Stop limiting yourself to customers down the block or around the corner. The world can be your oyster if you just stand up and dare to take your share. Think of your business not as a small company—but instead as a potentially giant firm in its early days of growth and development. Think of your business as one that is going to the top—one that will not be satisfied with anything else. And think of yourself as an entrepreneur with a taste for the luxuries of life—as one who will not be content with anything less than real wealth. Think like this and you'll no longer accept the crumbs.

Where can you turn once you have decided to tap the rich markets? Although there are excellent business opportunities all around you, there are two exceptional markets you should explore from the start: Uncle Sam and foreign trade.

Let's take first things first. When it comes to really huge and lucrative markets, the U.S. Government is the big daddy of them all. As the nation's largest single purchaser of goods and services, the federal government buys virtually everything private enterprise makes and sells. Each day, various government agencies solicit bids for a wide range of items from nuts and bolts to research reports, from paper clips to T-shirts. This mammoth shopping list totals many billions of dollars annually.

The surprising thing to many small business owners is that you can compete successfully for a piece of this pie, and to do so is a prime example of thinking big. The kind of thinking you need to rake in the really big bucks.

How do you go about snaring some big government contracts? To be eligible for most contracts, your firm's products must be listed on the so-called Qualified Products Lists. These lists, which are prepared by the various government agencies for their purchasing requirements, contain the products that have met certain essential specifications. The Qualified Products Lists are actually a sort of guarantee that the manufacturers listed on them can produce products according to set specifications.

Since the testing of your products to determine their suitability can be a time-consuming process, it is a good idea to have your products listed as soon as possible. This will enable your firm to bid on procurement contracts as they are announced and will guarantee your eligibility for all desired contracts.

Be aware, however, that listing on a Qualified Products List does not assure your firm of a contract award. It simply means your firm can deliver on the contract's specifications, and this enables the purchasing agency to consider the bid. A listing, in other words, allows the small company to compete for government business.

Listing involves these steps:

*The company's owner-manager or its technical expert (if there is one) should review Uncle Sam's specifications for the product category to determine whether the firm's products will meet the required performance or design standards.

*If it appears that the product is likely to pass required tests, management must apply in writing to the government agency for a qualified product listing. The letter (which must be forwarded with two copies) should include the number and date of the specification for which the tests are desired; the firm's brand designation for the product and the location of the plant where it is manufactured; and a complete description of the proposed testing facility.

In addition, a company applying for a listing must certify that it will abide by these requirements:

*That it will be bound by all terms and provisions in the document called, "Provisions Governing Qualification." Copies of this may be obtained from the government agency listing the product specifications.

*That the firm is the manufacturer or authorized distributor of the product.

*That the applicant will forward copies of actual test reports proving that the product conforms to listed specifications.

*That merchandise supplied for testing purposes is representative of standard production items.

*That a product which has failed the testing procedure will not be resubmitted until discovered defects are corrected.

*That a product listing will not be used for promotional purposes or to imply government recommendation.

*That the responsible government agency must be notified of any product changes once a listing has been obtained. Management must indicate whether such changes will interfere with the product's ability to meet qualification test requirements.

Although qualification testing is essential when required, some procurement contracts do not demand it. Agencies make the determination on a product-by-product basis. The final decision for each item is listed in sections three, four, and six of the specification form, which also tells the businessman where he can obtain the necessary information for getting a product qualified.

Qualified Product Lists are always open for inclusion of products from other manufacturers if all requirements are passed and proved to the appropriate agency. To take full advantage of this potentially lucrative sales outlet, small business management should list as many of its products as possible.

Up-to-date information on Qualified Products Lists can often be found in industry newsletters and trade magazines. In addition, the *Commerce Business Daily* (a U.S. Department of Commerce publication) carries notices of intent to establish a new list, and the expansion of the number of sources on an existing list. Write U.S. Commerce Dept, Washington, DC, 20233.

Another excellent way to keep up with government contract opportunities is to subscribe to a little-known yet extremely valuable service designed especially to help small firms compete for the federal dollar. Known as BEAM (BIDDERS EARLY ALERT MESSAGE), the service bridges the communications gap between federal agencies and owner-managers. BEAM is run by the National Small Business Association—a Washington-based organization active in the wide range of small business affairs.

BEAM's major feature is a nationwide data network geared

to disseminating government contract information. Before BEAM was launched, small business owners competing for government contracts were forced to rely on a single source of information—the *Commerce Business Daily*.

Crammed with in-depth contract information covering every federal agency, the *Commerce Business Daily* is the unabridged reference source on government buying. Published by the Government Printing Office, the paper lists as many as 600 categories of goods and services open to bids. The great bulk of this information is of little value, however, to individual firms.

Recognizing that busy owner-managers rarely have the time to sift through these massive listings, the National Small Business Association launched the BEAM service. By matching bidder capabilities with government requirements, BEAM provides customized information companies can act on.

BEAM subscribers simply indicate the kinds of contracts they wish to bid on. This data is then coded and entered into the BEAM computer system, where it is compared with similarly-coded information on available government contracts. When the codes match, a printout is issued to BEAM subscribers.

The printout keeps management up-to-date on government contract opportunities by providing the following information:

*Descriptions of all products and services that the government wants to buy and that the subscriber is capable of supplying.

*Technical specifications of the required items and where the products or services must be delivered.

*The official government contract number, the name of the government agency soliciting the bids, the deadline for requesting an official bid package, the closing date for submitting bids and the telephone number to call for additional information.

*Miscellaneous information, such as notification that the contract is limited to small businesses or regional bidders.

The success of the BEAM program is clear. Members have boosted combined government contract sales from roughly $80,000 per month to more than $4 million. Accurate and timely information has enabled small company BEAM subscribers to compete with the big boys for a substantial share of the government market.

You can think and sell big too. For starters, why not get more information on the BEAM program. Write the National Small Business Association, 1225 19th St. N.W., Washington, DC, 20036.

FALLING INTO A LEGAL TRAP:
How to prepare for new business laws

Laws. Laws. Laws.

Above all else, we live in a nation of laws. And for business, there is no exception: every company large and small is bound by a myriad rules and regulations. It is a good idea, in fact, to forget all you have ever heard about laissez-faire capitalism, for times *have* changed. Long gone are the days when free enterprise answered only to the laws of the marketplace. Today, legislative controls impact on every aspect of business operations from pricing to advertising.

It is, in fact, like wrestling with a legal octopus, and the struggle is getting worse all the time. In the past decade a flood of new legislation has streamed from the nation's capital—including some of the most comprehensive laws in history: the Occupational Safety and Health Act (OSHA), the Consumer Product Safety Act (CPSA), the Employee Retirement Income Security Act (ERISA).

The response from the small business community has been overwhelmingly negative. Entrepreneurs across the nation complain bitterly that just keeping up with the new legislation is a full-time job, and that assuring full compliance with the laws would leave little or no time to actually run their businesses.

"Just mention some of these laws to small business owners and they see red," says Herb Liebenson, Vice President of the influential National Small Business Association. "These men and women believe—and rightly so—that this legislation represents an impossible burden on small companies. They do not have the time, manpower or money to live up to some of the nit-picking mandates these laws require.

"A law like OSHA, for example, contains thousands of provisions regulating everything from the number of restrooms in a place of business to the acceptable sound levels. Although big corporations can and do hire teams of experts to deal with this legal behemoth, small firms have to do all the work themselves— and many are straining at the seams trying to keep up. For this reason, it is harder now than ever to run a small company successfully."

What then is the solution? Too often the solution is to take the easy way out—and that is really no solution at all. All too many entrepreneurs try to avoid the problem by simply ignoring the new laws, by making believe they do not exist. This strategy is based on the old mistaken logic that if you wish hard enough, all bad things will go away. That's only true in fairy tales.

In the real world, failing to pay full attention to the laws governing your business is a serious mistake indeed, and the consequences can be disastrous. Most of the tough new laws are no paper tigers by any stretch of the imagination. They are empowered with sharp teeth designed to assure implementation. The bottom line is this: failure to comply with some of the new laws can result in fines to the business owner of up to $10,000 and jail sentences to boot.

What's more, you can run into serious flack from consumer groups and labor unions. Just see what happens if you are convicted of selling or making dangerous products. Most likely, you'll be the target of every militant consumer group in the state—and this bad publicity may lead to a seriously-disruptive boycott of your firm. A single mistake could mean the end of your business.

What, then, is the solution? Obviously, trying to be an expert on each of the Occupational Safety and Health Act's 22,000 regulations is not the answer. Nor is it wise for a small business owner to take a stab at digesting all of the finer points of the complex Employee Retirement Income Security Act. There is just not enough hours in the day to do all of this and still run a business.

The wiser strategy, then, is to seek a happy medium. To recognize the power and the seriousness of the laws governing your business and to try and comply with them. But—and here is the important point—to base your compliance program on the most widely and frequently enforced aspects of the laws.

For example, when you know that a law like OSHA has 22,000 regulations, it makes the most sense to determine which of these provisions are most likely to be enforced by OSHA inspectors touring your facilities. You can probably isolate this information by questioning trade association experts and by speaking with business associates who have been subject to such legal inspections.

Although as a business owner you must and should stay in full compliance with all provisions of all relevant laws, knowing what the government is most interested in can help direct your compliance program. It can narrow the range of things you have to know to assure compliance and can make the job easier and faster. And more important, it can help you avoid those heavy fines, jail sentences and consumer boycotts.

I suggest that you launch your company's comprehensive legal compliance program by sitting down with a competent attorney and drawing up a master plan. Look closely at all the rules and regulations you must obey and set up a timetable to achieve full compliance promptly.

You may find it best for the purposes of smooth administration to tackle one law at a time. This way you will be less likely to confuse the various requirements and deadlines for compliance. To elaborate on this, let's take a closer look now at this crucial law we have been mentioning: the Occupational Safety and Health Act (OSHA).

One of the most far-reaching and detailed safety laws ever passed, OSHA is designed to protect employees from work-related accidents. Violations of the law may result in fines of up to $1,000 a day for every day the violation is not corrected. In addition, if a violation results in an employee's death, the owner or principal executive may be fined $10,000 and face a one-year jail sentence.

Obviously, you will not want to disregard a single provision: you will want to protect employees from accidental injury and protect yourself from heavy fines. Now is the time to make sure that you are in full compliance, because OSHA inspectors may visit your facilities at any time without prior notice.

The first step is to become familiar with the provisions that apply to your business. Help is available in gathering this information from several sources: your casualty insurance carrier, state or area trade association, a consulting safety engineer or your personal business attorney. The Federal Register, Part Two, contains full details on the regulations and how to conform to them. Copies of the Federal Register are available from the Occupational Safety and Health Administration, Washington, DC, 20210.

Once you are familiar with the law, initiate a two-part program to insure compliance. First, inspect your place of business for all existing and potential violations. It is a good idea to make up a checklist to be used for all future inspections. The task could be delegated to a responsible employee, who would simply be required to recheck all items on the list at frequent intervals.

Be sure to pay special attention to the more common and likely violations. Special surveys have revealed that these trouble spots often include equipment defects, lack of illumination of fire exit signs, objects that might cause employees to trip, improper mounting of fire extinguishers, exposed wiring, lack of hot water in washrooms and failure to display occupational administration posters.

After an initial inspection, the employer should start a program to correct existing violations. Get all the work finished quickly, and keep a detailed record of the progress that could be shown to an official if there is an inspection.

The second phase of a compliance program should be aimed at employees. It is considered important to educate them on the regulations. Employees who develop procedures to improve the work-safety environment will help cut down the accident rate. If they don't follow recommended procedures, the Administration will hold the employer at fault, even if proper equipment and tools were supplied to make a safe job.

To provide maximum protection, it is a good idea to perform the following: (1) post a copy of "Safety and Health Protection on the Job" on your bulletin board (this explains employee-employer responsibilities under OSHA, (2) advise employees that you are complying with Occupational Safety and Health Administration standards, and that they have an obligation to follow them at all times, and (3) meet with employees to discuss all particular regulations which apply to your business.

If you are inspected, tour your facility with the inspector. Afterward, he will advise you of any violations and inform you of a time limit for correcting them. Such an order must receive immediate attention. It makes good common sense, as well as business sense, to start a thorough program of compliance immediately. The sooner you act, the better your protection against fines and accidents.

To make your compliance effort easier, a training school established by the U.S. Labor Department helps small businessmen comply with the Occupational Safety and Health Act. Known as the OSHA Institute, the facility encourages voluntary compliance with the law.

The institute helps small businesses achieve legal compliance through a brief yet thorough training course. Instructors explain and analyze the act's provisions, showing entrepreneurs how the law applies to actual companies. To assure complete understanding of the law, the institute combines classroom instruction with practical training.

The institute, near Chicago, offers two major courses of interest for small businessmen. One, devoted primarily to the construction industry, is open to contractors, insurance carriers and safety engineers. The companion course, "A Guide to Voluntary Compliance", offers general industrial instruction for representatives of retail, manufacturing and service firms. The institute is equipped with teaching facilities that include closed-circuit television and a research library. Courses feature classroom lectures, equipment demonstrations, audiovisual presentations and application workshops. The learning environment has been designed to simulate business conditions.

The complete course for small businessmen requires one week of intensive study. Students attend seven one-hour classes a day and are expected to complete additional reading assignments at night. The extracurricular assignments are designed to broaden the individual's knowledge of specific provisions of the safety act and its applications.

Businessmen attending the institute are exposed to as many as 10 instructors during a one-week course. Instructors are experts in all major provisions, including fire prevention, plant safety and industrial hygiene. Classroom discussions center on each instructor's specialty, and the curriculum is planned to touch on all essential facts pertaining to compliance. In addition, students may question lecturers concerning the application of the safety act's provisions to business conditions.

Courses at the institute are free of charge. Students are responsible, however, for living, travel and miscellaneous expenses.

Interested businessmen may apply to the institute by writing to OSHA Office of Training & Education, Att: OSHA Training Institute, Washington, D.C. 20210. The letter of application should contain the owner-manager's name and address, firm name and address, principal line of business, preferred course of study, the reason for wanting to attend and requested dates of attendance (first and second choices). Application should be made at least a month in advance of attendance to compensate for waiting lists.

The Occupational Safety and Health Act has led many small businessmen to devote considerable time and expense to the maintenance of safe work facilities. The law's wide scope, however, leaves substantial margin for error, and even the conscientious owner-manager may fail to pass a Labor Department inspection.

The problem may be one of interpretation. Management, employees and inspectors may disagree over the meaning or intent of a legal requirement. The small businessman, therefore, may face a financial penalty or adverse judgment for what he believes is an unsubstantiated violation. If so, the businessman may present an argument to the federal "referee" on such disputes: the Occupational Safety and Health Review Commission, an independent agency of the executive branch.

If an inspector proposes penalties on alleged violations at a place of business and the employer feels this action is unjust, he may contest the findings within a 15-day period in a letter to the area director of the Labor Department.

The area director forwards this letter, within seven days, to the Review Commission in Washington, which assigns the case docket number, and informs the employer of a hearing date. The Review Commission assigns one of 41 judges (career civil servants) in nine key cities across the nation to preside over the proceedings and hear all arguments.

The hearing is the first stage of the Review Commission's two-part process for settling these disputes. The employer may be represented by a lawyer, although it is the obligation of the Labor Department to prove the businessman was in violation of the act. There are no court fees for the hearing, and no jury is present.

The judge's decision is forwarded to the three members of the Review Commission (members are presidential appointees who serve six-year terms).

Commission members review a case within 30 days of the hearing judge's decision. If they do not, the decision stands. If the case is reviewed, there is no time limit for announcing a final decision.

If the small businessman is not satisfied with the judge's decision, he may file a petition with the commission members for "discretionary review." This petition is a written brief stating the businessman's argument for a reversal of the decision. Although this may prompt the commission members to review the case, they are not bound to do so. They may simply take the petition under advisement, and fail to act on it.

A final decision by the Review Commission may be appealed through the U.S. Court of Appeals. If the small businessman decides to pursue this course, he is advised to enlist legal assistance.

The Review Commission is also open to complaints by employees or employee groups. For example, employees may contest the amount of time the Labor Department grants an employer to rectify a hazardous condition. In addition, employees may notify the Labor Department of alleged violations of the act.

Small businessmen seeking further information may contact a local Review Commission field office, or write to the headquarters office at 1825 K St, N.W., Washington DC, 20006.

Now you know some of your major rights and obligations under OSHA. Try doing the same for all other laws affecting your operation. You'll be safer and wiser for it.

BATTLING THE CONSUMER MOVEMENT:
How to anticipate and defuse consumer protests

Whoever said "There's nothing new under the sun," was, to put it bluntly, wrong. Throughout the course of history there are, from time to time, extraordinary new events and developments which rise to the surface with little or no warning. And once they do, life is suddenly different for all of us.

To business owners, this is no secret. Constant change, in fact, is a common thread which runs through every business. For entrepreneurs of the present generation, the greatest change of all is the rapid mobilization of the consumer movement. This single development has changed the entire fabric of business operations from advertising, to product planning to salesmanship. To business owners, therefore, there is something new under the sun: it is consumerism.

Although there have been stirrings of consumer unrest throughout the 20th century, only in the past two decades has this changed from primarily individual actions to a concerted effort. For the first time in history, business owners are faced with a unified consumer front—and a powerful one at that—composed of private organizations, myriads of government agencies and an active consumerist press. It's enough to make the early laissez-faire capitalists turn in their graves.

For modern-day business owners and managers the problem is local, state and national in scope. Virtually every town in the nation now boasts a consumer action group, most states have consumer interest bodies and on the federal level there are a number of agencies assigned to protect consumer interests.

The result of all of this concentrated attention on consumer affairs is a tough new set of restrictions on business practices. Some of these restrictions are legally enforced, others socially. In any event, the outcome is the same: every business large and small must now walk a thin line between ethical and unethical business practices. Failure to toe the mark can result in high fines, loss of business or even jail sentences.

How to deal with this pervasive development? That is the question! Well, while most business owners mistakenly thrash about moaning and complaining about consumerism, maybe there is a better way to deal with this phenomenon. What's the better way: look at consumerism as an opportunity in disguise—not as a problem at all.

Surprising as this may sound, it happens to make good business sense. For those who get super rich in this world usually do so by turning what the masses see as problems into opportunities. And in this case, it is quite easy to do. Rather than making the common mistake of fighting consumers tooth and nail, why not join the consumer movement yourself. After all, does it ever make good sense to do battle with your own customers? Of course not, whether the issue is consumerism or anything else, cordial relations, not friction, are what build sales.

Take a closer look at the consumer movement and you'll see that cordial relations are not really so hard to achieve. Because except for a small percentage of radicals, most consumerists are simple, working people asking only for a fair deal. They don't want to destroy the American system, burn your business or deny your profits. All they really want is honest, ethical treatment.

You can cater to this demand, avoid most consumer hassles and win a whole new set of appreciative friends and customers in the process. For while all the others are throwing verbal daggers at the consumerists, you can hold out the white flag. And that's exactly where the opportunity lies: as the only cooperative business around, you are sure to attract positive publicity and favorable notice among consumers themselves.

The best way to diffuse consumer protests is to anticipate them. To take the necessary actions designed to win over rather than turn off your customers. And the faster you act, the less likely your chances of running into a full-blown bout with consumer groups or agencies.

All you have to do is to eliminate those business practices most likely to generate consumer hostility, and institute special programs designed to show your sympathy with consumers' rights. Although you may not satisfy the die-hard activists, you will more than likely earn the trust, respect and patronage of the vast majority of your market.

The following is an *Eight Point Program for Cordial Consumer Relations:*

1. Design all advertising to be factual, informative and truthful in every regard. Never advertise "low-ball" prices to attract store traffic and then add on extra fees once the customer is in the store.

2. Adopt a reasonable and uniform policy on product returns. Instruct store personnel to accept returns in every case in which a product defect is obvious. In addition, allow customers to return unused and undamaged items for whatever reason is given.

3. Inform all your suppliers that you refuse to sell any dangerous, damaged or imperfect merchandise. Let it be known that any attempt to slip this type of goods by you will result in an immediate severance of the business relationship.

4. Notify your customers immediately of any communications you receive on dangerous or defective products sold through your outlet. Accomplish this through both paid advertising and press releases to be sure that all affected parties are informed.

In addition, immediately remove all existing stocks of the merchandise from the shelves.

5. Live up to the letter of all product and service guarantees offered by your business. Write the guarantees in plain and simple language, and clearly list all exceptions in bold print.

Also, make sure that your suppliers honor their warranties. Work with your customers in their attempt to obtain satisfactory treatment and refuse to carry the products of any manufacturer with a poor record of warranty performance.

6. Provide customers with a workable mechanism for voicing their gripes to you. A good idea is to set up a complaint box right at your place of business. Ask customers to submit any and all complaints on the way your business is run.

7. Respond to all consumer gripes with prompt remedial action. Study the complaints, determine if they have merit, and then correct the problem. This may require dismissing abusive employees, dropping profitable product lines or changing credit policies. Take whatever steps are necessary: in the long run, it will be well worth the effort.

8. Train your employees to work and act like professionals. This means making sure they are well-trained to provide comprehensive consumer information such as product specifications, warranty data, prices and durability. In addition, make sure your employees know how to smile and how to treat customers with courtesy and respect.

These few simple steps can get you started on the road to joining rather than fighting the consumer movement. It's a wise choice—and a profitable one too.

NEGLECTING PERSONAL FINANCES:
How to bolster your personal wealth

You know the old saying about being so busy watching the forest that you forget to notice the trees. Put simply, this refers to the tendency to get so wrapped up in a general theory or concept that the vital details are overlooked.

And this tendency is, unfortunately, typical of the way many independent business owners handle their financial obligations. As they struggle in the "battle zone," they neglect their "home front." Although many businessmen are thorough and conscientious when it comes to managing their company's books, they are lazy and in many cases ignorant of how to best safeguard their personal finances. The mistake they make is the failure to recognize that both are interrelated: personal financial success is crucial for an entrepreneur's business performance.

Why do we say this? Why does a big personal bank roll affect an entrepreneur's corporate performance? Why is it crucial to look through the forest and see the trees?

First and foremost it is important because financial reward is the greatest motivator of business performance. Behind just about every clever, hard-working business owner is the strong desire to get rich—very rich. And seeing this goal come within grasp—no matter how slowly—keeps fueling the entrepreneurial drive to the top.

If the entrepreneur is slovenly about his or her personal finances, all the work and effort will seem like nothing more than running in place—like getting nowhere fast. Although substantial sums of money may be earned, it can all come to naught if improperly managed. What happens then is predictable: the entrepreneur looks around, sees that all the sweat and dedication are adding up to nothing, and discouragement sets in. Discouragement leads to apathy, and that leads to a business on the way down.

Only an entrepreneur who sees the fruits of his efforts remains sufficiently motivated. Building a personal business is very much a two-pronged process: after the early formative period, every incremental spurt of business growth should be matched by a boost in personal wealth. All along the climb to the top the owner should see the concrete evidence of his developing personal fortune.

By neglecting the home front—by allowing personal finances to drift along unmanaged—the entrepreneur runs the high risk of losing the vast bulk of his earnings to inflation, taxes and poor investments. It is crucial, therefore, to take a constant interest in bolstering your personal wealth.

So keep in mind that for small business, the 70's is the decade of change. Fast and furious, legislation streams from the nation's capital, revising everything from tax laws to retirement planning to investment options. It is a full-time job just keeping up.

Staying up-to-date is a must. This is especially true in the sensitive area of money management: of all the hazards of self-employment, financial management tops the list. More than any other business threat, poor money management can have devastating effects on private and commercial holdings.

As we have said: for the self-employed, the challenge of money management is two-dimensional—personal and business finances demand equal attention. Ignoring one or the other is like building a house of cards: hidden faults can bring down the roof.

All too often, personal money management takes a back seat to the business side. Preoccupied with commercial interests, entrepreneurs fail to keep abreast of new developments in federal taxes, life insurance and estate planning. The outcome is predictable: staggering personal losses reduce or wipe away business gains. As a result, the self-employed work harder and harder just to stay in place.

"It's surprisingly true," says James Dagastino, a financial counseling executive with New York's Citibank. "Many successful business people are really bad at handling their own finances. They are usually too busy riding herd on business interests to cover the home front.

"Busy owner-managers should stick to the basics—municipals, blue chips and real estate. That's the best way to go when you don't have the time to supervise speculative investments. Anyone with a business to run cannot afford the luxury of sitting around all day watching the stock tapes."

The consensus among experts is clear: in today's volatile environment, wise money management means reducing the risks and seizing the opportunities. The following recommendations may be helpful.

Estate Planning: The orderly transfer of business interests— perhaps the biggest challenge to the self-employed—is a complex and demanding transaction. The best advice: prepare as early as possible. Poorly planned wills can set off years of family squabbling over the terms of an estate. Take the case of a merchant leaving a $75,000 estate composed primarily of a single retail shop. Under present laws, the owner may be wise to recapitalize the company to divide ownership between several heirs. Preferred shares with dividends may be divided equally among the heirs; common stock may be granted to the individual designated to run the company. This can pave the way for a smooth and equitable settlement.

Insurance: Inadequate insurance is another serious problem. Spiraling inflation and ever-higher jury awards have combined to swell liability settlements to record levels. One freak accident can jeopardize all personal assets. Years of business gains can be lost in a single law suit. The solution is clear: highly vulnerable individuals must step up insurance protection to maximum levels. Supplemental liability coverage, designed to cover risks excluded by other policies, is the first step. These so-called "umbrella policies" offer up to $1 million protection for little more than $100 per year.

Vulnerable Portfolios: The temptation to concentrate all investments in a single business or industry is strong—and in some cases presents a sound investment strategy. "Take the case of an auto parts dealer," Dagastino explains. "Knowing this business inside out, the individual naturally wants to invest in auto-related industries. So the dealer buys stock in his suppliers, distributors and the like. The problem is, this makes for a vulnerable portfolio. A reversal in the auto industry will have a negative impact on the dealer's personal and business interests. For this reason, the self-employed should spread investments across several industries in order to balance the cyclical patterns of each."

Trusts: Reducing the risks is only half the battle: capitalizing on the latest money-saving opportunities is equally important. This means ferreting out little-known yet highly attractive financial devices. One such device is a Clifford Trust. This arrangement enables entrepreneurs to cut the costs of their children's college by 50 percent or more. The procedure works as follows: the income from specially designed trusts is directed to the children, thus reducing taxes on the income. In many cases, the savings are adequate to cover a substantial percentage of tuition costs.

There is a lot to think about in the tax area. The newly enacted Tax Reform Act has changed the rules for all taxpayers, especially for self-employed individuals in the upper income brackets. Successful entrepreneurs will find there is a greater burden than ever on high earners, with many of the more popular tax-saving devices wiped from the books.

Most important, the trend toward "multiple write-off" tax shelters enabled taxpayers to invest in ventures designed to reduce taxes by more than the amount of the investment—up to three or four times the amount. Labeling most "multiple write-offs" as loopholes rather than legitimate investments, Congress has put tough new controls on the more exotic shelters including oil drilling, motion picture production and cattle feeding.

"The basic change is simple," says George Carter, a tax specialist with Merrill Lynch, Pierce, Fenner and Smith. "For the most part, investors can now write off only the amount of money they have 'at risk'—the actual amount invested. If an entrepreneur invests $25,000 in an 'at risk' tax shelter, $25,000 is the most the individual can write off. With multiple write-off shelters, a $25,000 investment may have produced a $75,000 deduction."

The change encourages investors to look for tax shelters with sound investment potential as well as beneficial tax treatments. Most shelters are no longer sufficiently attractive for the tax benefits alone. "Previously, the entrepreneur seeking a good tax shelter may have put $10,000 in a film production syndicate," Carter explains. "Thanks to multiple write-offs, this could produce a deduction of up to $40,000. The write-off alone made the investment worthwhile. Whether or not the film made money was of little consequence.

"Now that Congress has changed the rules, in most cases the same entrepreneur can write off no more than the amount of the investment—$10,000. If the taxpayer is in the 50 percent bracket, half of the total—or $5,000—is at risk in the deal. So the film has to have a good chance of making a profit in order to attract investors."

Still, even modified tax shelters can prove to be highly attractive for business owners. Take the case of an entrepreneur winding up an unusually prosperous year. The individual's first priority is to seek favorable tax treatment.

How is this done? Traditional investments, such as common stocks, are probably not the answer. A $10,000 investment in a blue chip stock, for example, offers no immediate tax benefits. Put that same $10,000 however, in a limited partnership in XYZ Oil and Gas Drilling and the full amount may well be written off immediately. For the 50 percent taxpayer, this is a $5,000 savings right off the bat.

Equipment leasing can be equally attractive. Here, short-term tax deferrals are the major appeal. Let's say a self-employed

...ssional approaching retirement age joins a limited partner-
... to purchase and lease railroad cars. The tax advantages
...olved enable the taxpayer to shield funds from taxation until
...tirement has occurred and the individual is in a lower tax
...racket. The result: significant tax savings.

A final note on the tax angle concerns the popularity of
municipal bonds. These investment vehicles enable high-bracket
earners to avoid taxation on their dividends. This can mean a
greater yield than savings accounts for many taxpayers.

The newest way to get some of this action is also the easiest.
Municipal Bond Funds enable you to get the tax-free dividends
without managing a bond portfolio yourself. All you have to do is
buy shares in the fund and the work is done for you (you do,
however, pay a small management fee for this convenience). It
may be a good idea to look over the prospectus of a bond fund to
see if the offer appeals to you.

Fidelity Municipal Bond Fund, 82 Devonshire St., Boston,
MA 02103.   800-225-6190

The Dreyfus Tax Exempt Bond Fund, 600 Lincoln Boule-
vard, Middlesex, NJ 08846.   800-325-6400

Chart 3 offers an indication of the comparative benefits of a
tax-free yield.

CHART 3

If your joint taxable income* is	Your income tax bracket is:	A tax-free yield of 5% 6% is equal to a taxable yield of:	
$24-28,000	36%	7.81%	9.38%
$36-40,000	45%	9.09%	10.91%
$64-76,000	55%	11.11%	13.33%
$100-120,000	62%	13.16%	15.79%

The most popular tax shelters are now packaged by brokerage houses and by other leading financial institutions. The

current favorites include ventures in real estate, equipment leasing and oil and gas drilling.

Taxpayers interested in the latest tax shelter plans can get all the details from competent bankers, stock brokers and accountants. As with all investments, it is a good idea to deal only with reputable parties and to read all the fine print before signing on the dotted line.

Remember, the fast-paced world of personal finance demands professional attention. For the self-employed especially, working with accountants or personal financial counselors is the best way to cover all the angles. Never make a major investment without professional advice.

NEGLECTING BUSINESS FINANCES:
How to bolster business income

Keeping an eye on personal finances is, to be sure, only half the equation. Knowing your way around a dollar is equally important in the business world, for sophisticated finances are at the heart of all modern businesses—large and small. Knowing how to use the latest tax breaks, accounting devices and investment vehicles for the benefit of your company is one of the best ways to assure success in today's highly competitive markets. It is one of the best ways to assure survival and prosperity in the business "battle zones."

And there is more to this than the straightforward accounting and financial principles set forward in previous chapters. As crucial as this is, sometimes the secret to really lucrative business ventures is learning the *little-known techniques* that can help you make and save more money. Money you can put to business or personal use.

In most cases, giant corporations and wealthy individuals have been cashing in on these techniques for years—getting rich and powerful on them while the vast majority of us never had a clue. Those days are over. Now you too can capitalize on some of the big money secrets the rich and powerful once had to themselves. The failure to take advantage of these techniques is a serious business blunder: what you fail to take for yourself, the competition will grab in an instant.

Making big money deals with small business dollars is not as farfetched as you may think. All you have to do is master the ins and outs of the money markets.

It is no secret that big money moves in privileged circles, tapping the most lucrative outlets for income and investments. Simple economics is the reason: big money has the muscle to demand the best terms. But clout isn't always essential. Small companies can make up with brains what they lack in brawn. Knowing the financial ropes can help even the smallest firms wheel and deal like the giants.

Take the exotic world of Treasury bill futures. Chances are that if you are a small business owner you have no knowledge of or experience with these very useful financial devices. It is about time you did. Put simply, Treasury bill futures are contracts to buy or sell federal Treasury bills. The bills are short-term money market instruments issued by the federal government at various yields. They can be used by companies to assure stable interest rates regardless of prevailing business conditions.

Here's how it works. Let's say a local entrepreneur builds up a successful auto dealership. Encouraged by the success, the owner decides to build a new outlet in a nearby town. Construction will begin in six months at a cost of $1 million.

Although the bank will likely approve the loan in advance, the terms will be based on the prevailing interest rates at the time the funds are paid. If the prime rate increases three points between the time of approval and the start of construction, the entrepreneur will be burdened with a major increase in debt service. The cost of the project will increase substantially.

The borrower can hedge against rising interest rates, however, by dealing in Treasury bill futures. If a five percent interest rate is acceptable to the entrepreneur—and Treasury bills for this yield are available—he can act in advance to assure this rate. This is done by obtaining a contract to sell federal Treasury bills at five percent at or near the date when construction is set to begin. Whatever happens to interest rates during the intervening months, the borrower will still be assured of paying five percent for the necessary funds.

For example, if interest rates climb from five to seven percent, the price of Treasury bills will drop two points (higher interest rates reduce the price of the bills) from 95 to 93. When the entrepreneur sells his futures for 95 (which the futures contract lets him do) and then buys them for 93, he has made a profit in his futures transactions. This profit makes up for the rise in interest rates which has occurred since the loan was first approved.

"The bad news is that the business owner must now pay the bank seven percent interest for the construction funds," says Kurt Hausafus, Vice President of the Chicago Mercantile Exchange. "The good news is that the profits from the futures transactions make up for the higher rates. In effect, the entrepreneur is paying only five percent for his money. And that's the beauty of Treasury bill transactions—they can hedge against interest rates."

Companies can also use Treasury bill futures to put idle cash to work at set interest rates. Owner-managers uncertain about future interest rates for large cash deposits can hedge against decreasing rates by using Treasury bills. The system is similar to that used for borrowing money.

"Treasury bills can be utilized by virtually every type of company including retailers, wholesalers, distributors and manufacturers," Hausafus adds. "Whether the firm is borrowing to build a new store, or just putting short-term cash to work, Treasury bill futures can be an important part of the company's finances."

Additional information on Treasury bills is available from the Chicago Mercantile Exchange—the central market for Treasury bill transactions—at 444 W. Jackson Blvd., Chicago, IL 60601.

In another winning device, small companies hungry for maximum profits can now turn idle cash into extra income. The trick is to dabble in the nation's money market funds.

Also, once the exclusive domain of corporate giants, money

market transactions are now practical for the little guy as well. Rather than face the market head-on, however, small firms limit their dealings to investments in money market funds. This approach allows inexperienced managers to obtain the benefits of money market transactions at limited risk.

Money market funds buy and sell investment vehicles such as government securities, commercial paper and certificates of deposit. The goal is to earn profits for both the fund and its investors.

All investment decisions are made by fund managers, most of whom are experts in money market instruments. Since all investment activities are handled by the fund, company managers don't have to keep up with daily transactions. There's no need to hire staff financial experts or to worry about maturity dates, rollovers or safekeeping. The fund does it all.

Here's how it works. Let's say a small contractor receives a lump sum payment of $47,000, half of which must be paid to suppliers in 20 days.

Rather than letting the sum sit idle in the company checking account until payment is made, management can put the cash to work in a money market fund. That way the money will earn interest from the day of investment to the day of withdrawal.

"Small companies can use money market funds as cash parking lots," says Charles H. Ross, Jr., President of Ready Asset Fund, a subsidiary of Merrill Lynch, Pierce, Fenner, & Smith. "Our dividend rates are comparable with bank rates but we pay out every day the money is invested with us. Unlike banks, we don't penalize for early withdrawals."

Money market funds are extremely liquid, providing investors with cash on demand. For this reason, cash reserves can collect dividends until the day they are needed. There are no long delays in converting money market investments into hard currency.

"We make it possible for small companies to tap the money markets safely and effectively," Ross says. "The stakes are simply too high for them to act alone. Some of the instruments we buy, for example, are sold only in $100,000 denominations and have fixed maturity dates. Few small companies can afford to tie up that kind of money.

"So we let them in on a scale they can afford. What's more,

we assume all the time and effort of managing the investment portfolio. Sure we charge a fee for this service—one half percent of the funds total assets—but we provide effective cash management in return. We put investors' cash to work right from the start."

There are a growing number of money market funds in the United States today. Most of them require that minimum investments be from $1,000 to $5,000 and that subsequent investments be in increments of from $500, to $2,000. Management fees also vary, depending on specific fund policies.

"The funds are becoming increasingly popular with the business community," says Ralph Richardson of the Dreyfus Liquid Assets Funds. "Companies turn to us because they want that extra dividend income we can provide. They want to take advantage of the float—that is making their money work until the instant it is needed."

Owner-managers interested in investments should compare at least two brokerage firms before making a final choice. Write or call their money firms for a free prospectus on each. That will provide you with in-depth information for making a wise investment.

What we are saying here is clear. Today, more than ever before, the business of business is money: how to make it, collect it, protect and invest it. The challenge has never been greater.

Sweeping changes in the business laws have put a new emphasis on financial expertise. Managers must now stay abreast of a whole new set of rules governing the tax laws, worker benefits and personal retirement plans. The complexities of a single new development, such as employee stock ownership trusts, can take months to master. So the bottom line is clear: to survive in this new age, entrepreneurs must be first-rate money managers.

Unfortunately, many small firms shy away from money management. This head-in-the-sand approach takes its toll: roughly 90 percent of small business failures are due to incompetent and ill-informed management.

A series of seminars launched by New York University may help stem the tide. Called "Financial Planning for Closely Held Companies," the seminars offer entrepreneurs a catch-up course on the latest developments in money management.

"Our market research tells us that the small business people need and want comprehensive training in modern business finance," says William Kulok, coordinator of the seminars. "We have talked with the self-employed in all parts of the country and most recognize the need for accurate and timely financial information.

"And that's where we come in. Most important, we offer exactly what small business people are looking for: a two-day cram course covering across-the-board financial developments. We know most managers have little time to devote to classroom work, so we design our programs to be fast, concise and to the point."

Seminars focus on the following subjects:

Taxes: This category includes power of appointment and establishing trusts.

Employee benefits: The emphasis here is on the Employee Retirement Income Security Act, individual retirement accounts, updating fringe benefits and deferred compensation.

Insurance: Financial discussions in this category include employee stock ownership trusts (which can be an excellent way to borrow corporate funds at low interest rates) and risk management.

Commercial appraisals: Participants learn how to appraise the value of their business interests. This can be helpful for maximum profits in business purchases, sales and mergers.

Most seminars run two full days with classes divided between lectures and group discussions. Specialists in the various fields of interest take turns in addressing the groups.

Seminars are held in various cities across the nation on a regular basis. The $485 fee, and the travel expenses to attend the sessions, are tax deductible. The costs are considered necessary to maintain and improve professional skills.

Further information, and a list of seminar locations, is available by writing the New York University School of Continuing Education, Division of Business and Management, 360 Lexington Ave., New York, NY 10017.

The ball is in your court. The next move is yours.

SELLING YOURSELF SHORT:
How to sell or merge
for windfall profits

Think about this one for a minute or two. What's the nicest thing about building a business from the simple seed of an idea into a formidable commercial success? What's the most rewarding thing about plowing your time, talent and finances into a company of your own and watching it grow from meager beginnings into a prospering enterprise?

Pride . . . Yes. Satisfaction . . . Yes. A sense of achievement . . . Yes. These are all, no doubt, significant rewards. To many entrepreneurs, however, these rewards are not enough—not sufficient compensation for the years of work, risk and sweat.

For these business owners, the nicest thing about building a business is—selling it. For them, all the effort is justified when the company itself is turned into a lump-sum cash settlement—a windfall profit for the owner.

And, we believe, this is the proper business outlook. Unless there is an heir for whom the business is being built, the owner should always be running the business with an eye towards its sale. Because the time may well come when the right combination of forces are acting to make the enterprise worth more on the auction block than in your hands. It may be that one chance in a lifetime to earn a windfall profit.

In the late 1960s, for example, America was swept with what I call "pollution fever." Ridding the nation of air, land and water pollution became the overriding goal of politicians, civic groups and millions of individual citizens. As a result, a myriad laws were passed to cut the flow of all kinds of pollutants into the environment.

In this almost hysterical atmosphere, companies providing antipollution products and services stood to profit handsomely from the increased demand for their output. As a result, these firms became the darlings of Wall Street and individual investors. No price, it seemed, was too high to pay for a share of a company in the environmental field.

And that's where Neil F. of Seattle, Washington comes in. A well-known engineer by profession, Neil had built up a respectable consulting firm (15 engineer-consultants) specializing in the previously-limited field of environmental systems. Suddenly, as the antipollution craze hit the business community, Neil's firm was inundated with engineering assignments. The professional staff grew from 15 to 36 and a new office was opened to handle the growing volume of business in and around Los Angeles.

To Neil—as bright a businessman as he was an engineer—the pride of watching his company soar in size was one thing: the realization that it was now worth a lot of money was, however, more important. Neil realized that the current wave of interest in environmental outfits would add several multiples to the market value of his firm—multiples that might not exist as the craze wore out.

Buy offers were coming in everyday, but Neil held out for the big one he knew would soon be surfacing. And it did. When a Chicago-based conglomerate with heavy interests in the construction field offered him $4.1 million in cash, Neil jumped at the offer and sold out. The figure was three times Neil's estimate of the firm's real value—a multiple he knew he would never see again. What's more, he was no longer a paper millionaire: his wealth was in cold cash.

The problem is, Neil's case is atypical. Why? Because most owner-managers make the all too common and tragic mistake of selling themselves short. They do not explore the profitable ways to sell and merge their companies. On the contrary, they see selling the business as the final act at the end of the business road. They view selling a personal business as simply a way to dispose of it when it is no longer wanted. And when this attitude prevails, its odds on that the owner is selling himself short.

Selling a business should be perceived as a time of great opportunity—and nothing less. A time to transform abstract wealth of capital assets, good will and market share into the only kind of financial wealth you can take to the bank: cash.

Just like investors in blue chip corporations, entrepreneurs must have access to a responsive market for the exchange of business interests. In time, after all, every business comes full circle—today's founder is tomorrow's seller. Call it expansion, retirement or speculation—owners must be free to sell out and move up. It is the basic building block of the system.

Salesmanship is the key: knowing how to promote, package and price the business is essential to attracting buyers. Proper presentation dresses the company up in its best suit and tie, focusing the spotlight on the most appealing attributes.

Experts recommend the following procedures:

Communications: The first step is to make the offer known, and to make it stand out amid the clutter of competing offers. Advertising is the name of the game: the more widespread the message, the more likely it will turn up a suitable buyer. Sellers can use any one or a combination of the following techniques: Newspaper ads, trade publications, word-of-mouth through industry contacts, business brokers.

Business Brokers: In many cases, the use of business brokers is the most productive approach. Brokers know the ropes—they are best equipped to move a company to sale quickly and profitably. Sellers do, however, pay for this advantage: brokers retain 10 percent or more of the selling price as commission.

Still, the brokerage commission is often a worthy investment. Brokers earn their fees by tapping a wide network of business contacts; assessing and screening potential buyers; and negotiating a valid contract suitable to both parties. In short, brokers boost the chances of selling the business and then reduce the red tape in the ensuing transactions. (Bankers, attorneys and accountants can usually recommend the names of qualified brokers.)

Handling the Details: The seller should do the following to protect personal and business interests during the course of negotiations:

Work with a competent attorney and escrow agent.

Package vital business records—such as profit and loss statements and balance sheets—for study by the potential buyer.

Be sure that prospective buyers have the necessary capital and credit to make the purchase.

Notify creditors of the intention to sell and have them clear bills through the escrow holder.

Pricing: When it comes to selling a business, few owners really know how to figure the price tag. Too many factors must enter the equation: sales, earnings, risk, potential, security, taxes, goodwill. Confusion usually reigns: how do you value each?

The following formula provides some answers.

FORMULA FOR SELLING A BUSINESS

1. To arrive at a fair market value for most small companies, first determine the adjusted tangible net worth (the value of all current and long-term assets less liabilities).

2. Estimate how much a buyer would earn annually with an amount equal to the tangible net worth if invested elsewhere.

3. Add to this a reasonable salary for the owner-operator.

4. Determine the average annual pre-tax earnings of the business over the past few years.

5. Subtract the total of earnings and reasonable salary from the average net earnings figure. This gives the company's extra earnings power.

6. Multiply the extra earnings figure by a factor of five or more for well-established firms; by three for moderately-seasoned companies; and by two for young but profitable outfits.

7. Compute the final price as the adjusted tangible net worth plus the value of intangibles.

Although this formula is not a universal solution to business pricing, it does provide a workable guideline for setting fair market values. Before establishing a firm price, however, it is a good idea to review personal financial considerations, check the tax implications and consult with a professional.

If selling out is not your cup of tea, mergers may be. Mergers and acquisitions offer small companies unlimited opportunities for business expansion. By merging with large and successful firms, entrepreneurs may tap large sources of capital.

When capital supplies are tight, mergers and acquisitions may be the only means for small firms to attract enough cash for future growth. Parent corporations are often willing to provide subsidiaries with the large amounts of money banks and venture capitalists are reluctant to risk.

Mergers and acquisitions have gained added significance in recent years as other key capital sources have all but dried up. Wall Street, for example, has been cold to small company stock offerings and major lending institutions have shied away from funding new ventures. This has forced hundreds of small firms to apply the brakes on further expansion.

Entrepreneurs impatient with the nation's capital markets have turned instead to actively seeking mergers or acquisitions. By selling out to large corporations, owner-managers have been able to raise substantial cash without delay.

Approximately 2,000 mergers are completed every year. The deals involve companies of all sizes, legal structures and business specialties. Reasons for the mergers also vary: some are designed to benefit the company and others are intended to boost the owner's personal finances.

Benefits to the acquired company are clear: new cash investments and added management controls may fuel continued growth. And owners gain by collecting a considerable amount of cash or stock from the sale. Depending on the terms of the agreement, entrepreneurs may stay on to manage the firm or may leave once the merger is complete.

Owner-managers interested in seeking mergers should act

from a position of strength. This means negotiating only when sales and profits are at peak levels. Healthy companies can demand selling prices of from 8 to 13 times net after-tax earnings or from 1 to 2½ times book value.

Finding an interested buyer can, however, be a frustrating experience. Most large corporations are inundated with thousands of offers and can afford to select only the best prospects. The competition to attract a good buyer is therefore intense.

Help is available from consulting firms specializing in mergers and acquisitions. For a set fee ranging from 3 to 7 percent of the selling price, consultants will help you search for a qualified buyer. They will analyze your corporate needs, recommend legal counsel and appraise merger proposals. The service is a helpful aid for companies seriously interested in exploring the merger market. Names of reputable consultants may be obtained from business attorneys, trade associations or commercial bankers.

Before the decision is made to seek a profitable merger or acquisition, it is a good idea to have an accurate estimate of your company's worth. This can be arranged by contracting with one of the well-known firms specializing in the appraisal of business enterprises. Known as "commercial appraisers," these outfits can tell you:

> *What assets actually exist
> *The age, condition and utility of existing assets
> *The value of the assets
> *Potential tax liabilities
> *Potential accounting depreciation charges.

The valuation can also indicate which way to structure your merger or acquisition agreement for the greatest financial return. Various types of arrangements include "cash for assets," and "stock for stock with pooling treatment."

> You can write for a free booklet on the various types of merger deals to Marshall and Stevens, Inc., 600 S. Commonwealth Ave., Los Angeles,

CA 90005. 213-385-1515. This major appraisal
firm maintains offices in other large cities as
well (check your white pages).

The same psychology that operates with selling a going
concern also applies when it comes to mergers and acquisitions.
That is, the owner-manager must be sure not to sell his company
short. The appraisal gives some concrete indication of the firm's
worth, but the rest is up to you. You must use every factor in the
company's favor to drive up the merger terms, or acquisition cost,
in your favor.

You must be prepared for this, principally by tapping the
merger and acquisition markets only when your company is
especially hot. Just like Neil's engineering outfit became an
instant star in the early days of environmental activism, it is more
than likely that this kind of go-go climate will sooner or later
affect your industry as well. And that's when you'll want to strike:
when potential suitors are tripping all over themselves for a piece
of your action.

This kind of frantic activity took place recently in the wine
industry. As wine sales started moving up all the corporate sales
charts, the big beverage and food conglomerates moved in to
gobble up all the independent wineries. The giants knew a
growth industry when they saw one, and most of the leading
firms, like Coca Cola and Pepsi, bought in fast. The rush meant
big bucks—many millions in stock and cash—for the once-
ignored vineyards.

Even Heather F.'s Maison Estates, one of the smallest
producers in California's burgeoning wine region, found itself a
hot, sought-after property by at least a dozen west coast food
and/or beverage concerns. Although Heather, a 33-year old
MBA and former housewife from Indiana, had originally
planned to keep her vineyard for life, the sudden smell of
windfall profits was too lovely to resist.

Her plan of action: to sell out at the greatly-exaggerated
prices being offered to her for an acquisition, pocket the cash
profits, and stay on to manage the vineyard as a highly-paid
executive of the parent company.

And that's exactly what she did: "I simply called my banker and asked him to set up a meeting with the president of Cranklee Foods. This was the largest company bidding for Maison Estates, and I figured it would come up with the best acquisition terms in the end," Heather notes.

"I was right. I asked for $3.7 million—expecting all along to get no more than $2 million. But—surprise of surprises—when they heard my terms they came back with $3.3 million and we settled for $3.5. That's $3 million more than I paid to launch the firm four years before."

A handsome profit—and that was only the appetizer. Heather remained president of what was now Cranklee's Maison Estates division, retained a good deal of operating authority and enjoyed a long-term contract calling for $110,000 per year plus bonuses for exceptional performance.

"Arranging an acquisition at the right time brought me the best of both worlds: personal wealth and business clout with virtually no financial risk. That's flying first-class."

WEARING ALL THE COMPANY HATS: How to overcome the "superman syndrome"

Let's call a spade a spade. In business, you have two basic choices. To remain a small, unassuming operation or to aim for continued expansion. Either you have it in your blood to run a big, profitable company or you are content with a small and informal operation.

If you find yourself standing squarely on the side of money and power—if building a commercial dynasty is definitely your desire—than you had better start preparing now for one of the major adjustments ahead: letting others share in the management of your business.

There are no two ways about it. To establish a really huge business enterprise, the owner-manager must relinquish some of the day-to-day chores to competent subordinates. Remember, the bigger your ship the larger the crew and more officers you'll need. You can't be swabbing the decks when you should be planning and supervising major strategy.

It's true: in the real world, "supermen" only wind up exhausted trying to do it all. The real winners have the smarts to surround themselves with the best managers money can buy.

And that's exactly where most small business owners and

managers fail to measure up. Chained by quirk or habit to the old "I'll do it all myself" psychology, they never graduate from the meager "mom and pop" type business perpetually scratching along for a marginal profit. And that is a shame because virtually every small business, if properly and courageously managed, can transform itself into a commercial giant. The secret is to avoid the common mistakes.

When it comes to business expansion, most small business owners trip up in the area of work delegation. Caught up in the so-called "superman syndrome," millions of unsuccessful entrepreneurs believe that they alone must handle every single business activity. The secrets of the business, therefore, remain trapped in their heads. Not a single employee is privileged to the skill and experience the owner-manager could and should share with top people in his staff.

What does this mean? Simple! With one person alone knowledgeable about the business, how big can the company grow? Not big at all. Because no one person really is superman—no one person can possibly build and manage a true industrial giant. In big business, there's really no such thing as a one-man show.

Moving away from the superman syndrome means moving towards effective delegation of corporate power and responsibility. It means hiring a capable staff, smart and ambitious enough to help push the company through the tough stages of early growth, and to keep it headed, ever stronger, for the top.

The best approach is to follow the example of the well-known Fortune 500 giants like IBM and Xerox. Companies which have revolutionized the business world and trounced all competition by putting in place top-flight personnel organizations and then lighting a fire under their people to go out and shake up the world. Imagine Xerox trying to grow from its meager beginnings to its present status if one "would-be superman" insisted on making every sale and designing every product himself. It could never have happened.

What's more, hiring a capable staff makes the owner a better manager in the process. Gives you more time to determine the company's overall business strategy, to spot the major trends and to plan for the future. Getting bogged down with petty details is no way to build a giant.

How then do you plan personnel needs? How do you hire and motivate top employees? How do you delegate power on a rational and orderly basis? The following guide to manpower management may help you accomplish all of the above:

*Use sound business projection techniques (see Chapter 6) to anticipate future business volume. Based on these assumptions, determine the number of employees required to handle the workload six months and then one year from the date of the projection.

*Activate the hiring process 45 days before the needed employees are actually required on the job. Prepare a job description for each slot to be filled, including work responsibilities, salary range and required skills. Use this information to work with employment agencies, free state labor services and in writing help wanted ads.

*Once the staff grows to ten or more employees, prepare a formal organization chart clearly illustrating the lines of responsibilities and authority. (A sample is shown in Chart 4.) This is crucial: the existence of an organization chart makes it perfectly clear who is responsible to whom. There can be no question about the lines of authority.

*Make the company a two-way street. Ask employees to communicate with you openly and freely. This will help keep your ear to the ground in terms of employee gripes and ambitions and will help you make the kind of key policy decisions expected of you.

In addition, employees can be the best source of information pertaining to the future growth of the firm. They are in the best position to advise you of developing manpower needs: when to expand the organization and put new employees into place to handle the growing workload. Unless your staff is flexible enough to respond quickly to soaring business requirements, you will find the company's growth is stunted simply because there are not enough people on hand to satisfy customer requirements.

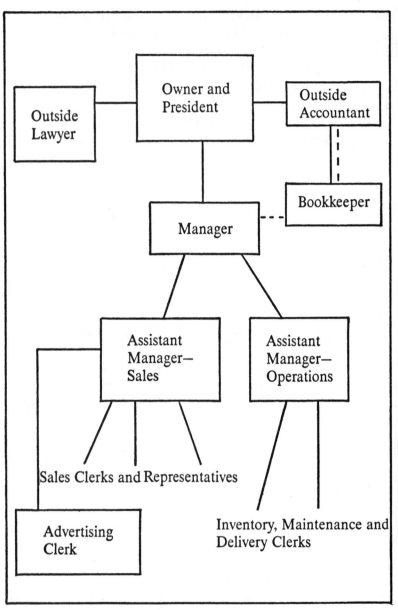

CHART 4

SAMPLE OF TYPICAL ORGANIZATION CHART
FOR SMALL BUSINESS

*Encourage maximum motivation and productivity by designing a company-wide cash-paying incentive program. Leave no one out, but make the largest awards to those with the greatest impact on bottom line profits. This way every single employee will share a stake in the firm's success and that is the best way to breed loyalty and motivation throughout the company.

*Pay the cash incentives twice a year for every six month period in which the company boosts sales and profits by 20 percent or more. Award employees according the following formula:

> TOP MANAGERS: 12 percent of annual salary
>
> TOP SALES REPRESENTATIVES: 10 percent of annual salary
>
> SALES CLERKS: 6 percent of annual salary
>
> TOP OPERATIONS STAFFERS: 5 percent of annual salary
>
> UNSKILLED EMPLOYEES: 3 percent of annual salary

Always make it perfectly clear that these awards will not be paid whenever the company does not boost sales and profits by the minimum 20 percent figures. Tieing the incentives to performance is the only way to boost productivity.

*A final word: put sales representatives on commission and allow their earnings to be open ended. Any sales ace good enough to pile up commissions to the sky is earning you big money. Don't put a limit on his earnings and he won't put one on yours. When you have a tiger on the loose, let him run.

"I heard about this program at Harvard University which matches up interested MBAs with jobs in small businesses," says Lewis P., owner of a fast-growing food brokerage concern selling a wide variety of dairy products to midwest supermarket chains. "So I made contact with the placement office and hired one of the school's top graduates. Lucky for me he preferred a small business career rather than taking a job with one of the 30 or so big corporations bidding for his talent.

"After a few weeks on the job I could see his extraordinary

sales talents and this convinced me to give up the reins and let some one else take on some customers. Man, did he do a job. In just four months he brought in a case of orders worth to the tune of $711,000 in sales. Adding up his commissions, he was making money at the rate of $182,000 per year. But that was fine by me. My profit from his work was twice that figure and all I had to do was sit in the office and cash my checks.

"I've learned my lesson: when you have a good employee, let him go the distance."

NONCOMPETITIVE PRICING:
How aggressive pricing can edge out the competition

All really wise businessmen in history have shared a common insight: the recognition that pricing and competition go hand in hand; that business is a contest between competing factions—and that aggressive pricing has a lot to do with naming the winner.

Not a traditional type of contest to be sure, but a contest nevertheless. A contest of competing products and services all battling one another for an ever-greater share of the consumer's dollar. Making it big in business means winning this contest—taking first prize in the competitive sweepstakes.

The truly wise entrepreneurs have shared another key realization: that aggressive pricing is one of the best weapons for winning sales away from the competition. They have recognized that pricing is much more than simply a way to value merchandise—it is that and much, much more. Effective pricing can be used to boost sales, destroy competitors and dominate a market. That's power.

Let's take a closer look at the mechanics of pricing. As a business owner, you set your own prices for products and services. These prices go on to become the most visible parts of your company. In most cases, in fact, they play a vital role in your firm's very survival. That is because price is one of the key factors consumers consider when making a purchase—one of the crucial things they look at when choosing your offering from those of the competition. For some consumers, price is the utmost consideration.

Unfortunately, many small business people make the fatal mistake of never questioning how the prices they set stack up against the competition. Are they higher or lower? If higher, is there a product quality justification for this? Do consumers perceive this justification? Or do they simply think of you as overpriced? Would a slight drop in prices win over thousands of new customers? Without this questioning and analysis, how do you know if you are really competitive? How do you know if you are grabbing every opportunity to take away business from the competition and dominate the market singlehandedly?

Frankly, without this analysis, you don't have answers to any of these questions. You are in the dark concerning your own competitiveness. You are waging the business contest with one hand tied behind your back. That is something the really successful capitalists would never do. Never.

The solution to this problem is to adopt a policy of "aggressive pricing." First and foremost, you must initiate a systematic strategy for setting your prices: a strategy that assures you of a decisive advantage over the competition. Your goal at all times is to take the offensive—grab the lead and set the pace.

Most important, remember that the pricing mechanism is an ongoing business function to be done monthly, weekly or even daily if necessary. You must keep up-to-the-minute on all market conditions and capitalize on every opportunity to seize the advantage. That's aggressive pricing.

To base as vital a function as pricing on a half-hearted effort is asking for trouble—and in nine out of ten cases it's trouble you will get. The tendency to set noncompetitive prices forces thousands of companies to operate at a severe disadvantage, and causes others to visit with the bankruptcy judge. All too many business owners set prices according to generalized industry standards while others put all of their faith in manufacturers' recommendations. Both policies are simply bad business: pricing is too important to let others decide for you. Too important to even let others know what you are doing until you have acted. When it comes to aggressive pricing, secrecy is also crucial.

As owner and manager, you and you alone are responsible for setting your company's prices. To do so, you should take into account a number of key variables. The type of business you operate, for example, has a major impact on your pricing strategy. The ideal markup percentage usually varies from a low of roughly 20 percent in self-service food stores to a high of 50 percent in fashionable clothing shops.

In many instances, the difference in markup percentages for various industries is based on risk factors. Toy retailers must order their wares well in advance of the sales season, gambling that the choices they make in the spring will be popular at Christmas. In a fickle and fad-oriented business like children's toys, that is a big gamble indeed. For this reason, toy merchants must score with a big markup on the winners they do pick. Be sure to take a high markup if you are in an equally-risky business.

But let's get back to the nitty-gritty. Aggressive pricing is a responsive, flexible pricing strategy designed to capitalize on current market conditions, throw the competition off balance and command the lion's share of the market.

How is this done in practice? Well, let's say you are dealing in a "parity" business—that is a business in which products and services are very much alike. Considering the similarity of merchandise, consumers will often base their selections on the store or product with the lowest prices. A discount of as little as five or ten percent, for example, will often sway the vast majority of consumers to give up traditional shopping patterns and switch to where the savings are.

In spite of this great opportunity to suddenly dominate the market, most merchants and manufacturers in parity industries are willing to maintain identical prices. All are trapped by the fear of being the trend setter—the pricing predator.

So you see that aggressive pricing can be used as a sales

magnet. It is a weapon for stirring up the market and drawing more of the sales to your company. Even if others then turn around and imitate you—like also lowering their prices—they are too late. By acting first—by being the aggressor—you and you alone have earned the reputation as a discounter. Consumers think of you when they think of bargains.

Aggressive pricing is not, however, limited to discounting. The strategy can be used with equally good results in raising prices as well. Again, it is a matter of monitoring market conditions and taking the initiative to break away from the pack.

In a very good example of this, hundreds of retail stores were carrying a new low-priced perfume imported from South America. In spite of a nice fragrance and attractive packaging, the product was not selling well at all. It was, in fact, a real dog.

That's until an alert merchandising manager at one of the major stores handling the product noticed that while this low-priced perfume was not moving, the expensive brands were doing very well. He had the thought maybe snob appeal was at work here, and therefore simply doubled the price on the South American brand. Thanks to a little promotion touting the product as "expensive," sales took off for the first time. While the store had sold three dozen bottles a week at the old prices, it tripled this volume at the new $12 price.

Of course news spread quickly and other retailers joined the price raising scheme. But too late. The pricing predator had already rung up hefty sales. Then as a double strategy, that same merchandising manager lowered the price again to $10 while all the others settled on the $12 ticket. Since the brand was now in demand, consumers were happy to visit the original store for a price break. A little heads-up pricing beat the competition cold— and beat them twice.

"We used the strategy of aggressive pricing with incredibly good results," raves Hugh G., owner of a thriving chain of yarn and pattern shops. "As everyone knows, needlepoint recently became a very popular hobby. As a result, we were suddenly faced with intense competition in markets we used to have pretty much to ourselves.

"Rather than trying to squeeze out a small share of these

markets, we decided to lower our markup below the industry standard, and lower our prices accordingly. As the most-established stores around, we were able to absorb the lower prices far better than the others.

"To make a long story short, the competitors kept their prices high and we walked away with a big chunk of their business. When they finally decided to reduce the markup, it was too late. A good number of the firms bailed out and we were back dominating the markets again. Our hip pricing strategy actually caused a shakeout in the markets and wound up boosting our sales and profits by more than 60 percent."

You can't argue with success.

IGNORING THE EXPORT CRAZE:
How to make a bundle
selling abroad

A famous American, advising young people on the secret of success, uttered the now-famous words: "Go west, young man, go west."

Believe it or not, that advice still holds true for the nation's entrepreneurs—but with an added dimension. Today, one secret to success is to go east, north, south—and west, to sell your products and services to all the burgeoning markets across the globe.

In our ever-shrinking world, exporting is no longer the reserve of giant corporations. Thanks to startling advances in technology, the gulf of time and space between nations has been greatly reduced. Now, even small and mid-size companies can reap tremendous profits in the export markets. The world can be your oyster—all you have to do is to open your eyes to the opportunities all around.

The proof is in the pudding: hundreds of entrepreneurs have racked up millions of dollars of personal profit selling everything from simple machines to books to children's shoes to developing and industrialized nations in all parts of the world.

"My experiences with the export market have been nothing

short of phenomenal," says Arlene L. of Boston, Mass. "In my very first export deal, I made more money than I'd ever made in my life. I bought the rights to a brick-making machine that was already obsolete in the U.S., but was considered a modern miracle in a tiny backward country in the Pacific. So the same rights I paid $2,200 for in the states I turned around and sold to that country for $1,200,000. It made me an instant millionaire."

Although this kind of success doesn't happen everyday—it does happen to many business owners savvy enough to explore every opportunity. The problem is, most small companies mistakenly shy away from the export markets, believing them to be too costly and complex for small operators. This is not true. A number of services are now available to help entrepreneurs tap the riches of foreign markets. All you have to know is where to look for help—and that is exactly what we will show you. So stop making the mistake of ignoring the export markets—it's a mistake that may be costing you millions.

Professional assistance is now available for small firms seeking to expand into foreign markets. Spurred by a lagging national trade balance, the Commerce Department, for example, has launched many programs to advise the U.S. exporter. And in the private sector, specialized consulting firms can help the small company plan and implement complete export programs.

The private consultants, known as export management companies, have become increasingly popular as a growing number of small owner-managers, lured by the prospect of substantial profits, are willing to face exporting's potential problems. And it makes good business sense: export markets are large and often growing.

Once the decision has been made to take the giant step to foreign trade, the owner-manager should contact an appropriate export management company.

A key to success is selecting the private consultant best equipped to meet the small company's needs and objectives. The Commerce Department estimates there are from 600 to 1,000 export management companies in the U.S., ranging in size from a single consultant to major professional outfits with numerous offices and hundreds of employees.

The best way to contact virtually every major company is to write to the Federation of Export Management Companies, P.O. Box 7612, Washington, DC 20044. Owner-managers should include a brief letter outlining the firm's export objectives and at least eight copies of product or company brochures. The federation will distribute the material to its regional members.

"When we, for example, receive information on a firm from the federation, we determine if any of our local EMC's are willing to take on the company as a client," says an official of the National Association of Export Management Companies, a New York-based regional trade association. "If interest is expressed, we bring both parties together for the initial discussions.

"It is quite possible, of course, that the owner-manager's letter to the Federation will yield a positive response from EMC's across the nation. If so, the small company's management will have to choose among a group of potential consultants. Although the final selection should be based on a wide variety of factors, there are a few well-established criteria for making the proper choice."

The officials recommendations include these considerations:

Competing Products: The consultant should not be representing a competitor's products in the export market.

Complementary Products: It is often beneficial to the client firm to be represented by a company experienced in handling a product closely related to its own. The small manufacturer of automobile seat covers, for example, will probably do well with an export management company selling noncompeting auto equipment to foreign buyers.

Sales Staff: The owner-manager should know the size of the company staff and the ratio of representatives to clients. A one- or two-man sales force may not be able to offer a new client sufficient attention.

Client Roster: A good deal of information often can be gleaned from a list of existing clients. Are they successful, well-known firms? Are they generally large or small? Are they technical or product oriented?

The client company's major responsibility ends with the selection of an export management company. The consulting firm then takes over the entire export function. It purchases the company's products at a discount price and sells them in export markets for a profit.

The discount to the consulting firm is subject to negotiation, but it generally ranges between 10 and 20 percent below whole-sale. The actual price must, of course, enable both parties to cover overhead and earn a reasonable profit.

If the export program is a success, the small firm may eventually terminate the relationship and hire a staff expert. Once the company's products have gained acceptability and a substantial sales volume, an in-house export department will be economically feasible and increasingly profitable.

Another excellent source of export assistance is the Commerce Department itself. International trade specialists, for example, are based at Commerce Department field offices across the country. Their job is to promote American exports by helping local business firms develop and maintain successful export programs.

A firm requesting export assistance is advised to contact the Commerce Department's nearest business service office. A trade specialist will act as the company's export consultant, working closely with the owner-manager and even visiting the firm. He will remain in constant communication until the firm is prepared to handle its export program itself, after which he may call occasionally to check on the company's progress and ask if more help is needed.

"Since small and medium-sized firms generally require the most assistance to avoid the pitfalls of exporting, we concentrate a lot of our efforts toward helping this category of company," says an export specialist at the New York business service office. "They can rarely afford to hire experts in this field, so we try to give them all the help they need for success. Our work cuts down on the more time-consuming tasks involved in exporting, thus freeing the company's management for other responsibilities."

The specific export programs and services available to small businessmen include the following:

World trade data report: The data reports are actually financial statements on foreign firms, providing management with some knowledge of the firms with which it will be dealing. Potential agents, distributors and the like are no longer unknown entities. Reports are obtained within 30 days of request.

Agent-distributor service: One of the major problems facing a potential exporter is the search for a suitable foreign distributor. Through its agent-distributor service, the Commerce Department will help an American firm obtain an agent or distributor abroad. The process is completed within 30 days.

Trade list: Each list includes the names of agents, distributors, importers, and dealers handling a particular commodity in a specific country.

World trade center shows: The shows are designed to help American exporters present their products to foreign buyers. Held at the Commerce Department's trade centers in key cities around the world, the shows normally feature one commodity at a time. American firms are invited to participate in the shows, or may petition the department for exhibit space.

World trade fairs: The U.S. often will construct a major pavilion at an international trade fair in order to provide exhibit space for American exporters. The fee for display space at the fairs varies according to a number of factors, including booth size.

Joint export expansion program: The Commerce Department will often assist a small group of American firms wishing to hold a miniature trade center show. The group, composed of from four to eight firms, will be entitled to use of a trade center for a mutual display of their products.

Embassy assistance: The Commerce Department will arrange for U.S. embassies to assist American businessmen visiting foreign nations. Traveling alone, or with a trade mission, the businessmen receive help in arranging meetings with local industry leaders and other contacts. The department requires a minimum of three weeks' notice to secure the necessary arrangements.

Any further information, including fees, specific dates, locations, and trade show applications, may be obtained from any Commerce Department field office or by writing to the Commerce Department, Office of International Trade Promotion, Washington, DC 20230.

Once you have your feet wet in the export market, you may find that routine credit problems may be compounded for small firms selling in the export market. With collections international in scope, management must learn to deal with various languages, currencies and payment forms.

The commitment to sell in overseas markets must be matched by an equal determination to collect on all receivables. Failure to obtain payment on a small percentage of orders threatens the firm's financial stability and seriously erodes cash flow. Small companies must rely on careful planning to collect on overseas accounts. Resorting to aggressive tactics once problems develop is generally expensive and ineffectual. The idea is to establish rigid credit criteria, to make no exception for credit approvals and to select appropriate payment forms.

Familiarity with the following methods of international payment will help management devise effective collection procedures:

Cash in Advance: This method eliminates collection problems and offers the exporter immediate use of receivable funds. It also reduces the exporter's administrative expenses and improves cash flow figures. Overseas firms are unlikely, however, to accept cash in advance terms unless pressured to do so. Customers generally prefer to retain funds in interest-bearing accounts for as long as possible and are also hesitant to issue payment before delivery. Exporters must, therefore, accept alternate payment forms.

Open Accounts: This enables customers to charge continuous purchases against a line of credit. Although payments are requested upon delivery of merchandise, a partial balance may remain open for 90 days. Because this liberal credit policy is risky for the exporter, the plan should be offered only to customers with superior credit ratings.

Consignment Sales: Products furnished on consignment are not paid for at the time of delivery. Instead, overseas customers are allowed to defer payment to the exporter until the merchandise has been resold. Although not an ideal payment plan, this arrangement may at times be preferable to losing a major or potentially-lucrative account. Consignment sales should not, however, be authorized in economically or politically unstable nations. In addition, the exporter must demand a contractural agreement establishing liability for the property until it is sold.

Letter of Credit: It is a frequently-used form of collection in export transactions. The credit document, issued by a bank at the buyer's request, promises to pay the seller a specified sum of money upon receipt of cargo delivery papers. Although letters of credit may be revocable or irrevocable, the exporter should insist on the latter. This means that once credit has been accepted by the seller, it cannot be altered in any way by the buyer.

Small exporters must minimize risk conditions, so the owner-manager should insist that the letter of credit be confirmed through a U.S. bank, which makes it responsible for payment regardless of the financial condition of the buyer or the foreign bank.

Additional information on export payment forms may be obtained from international banking departments or from any U.S. Department of Commerce district office.

You will be happy to know, however, that regardless of your collections or other problems, Uncle Sam will share some of the risks with you.

Export-Import Bank: Services now available to U.S. exporters through the Export-Import Bank share responsibility for the rising interest in foreign trade. The bank fosters export activities by protecting companies from some commercial and political losses overseas.

Eximbank's key service is a form of insurance designed to cover exporters in the event of non-payment by foreign customers. If buyers fail to pay either for commercial or political reasons, Eximbank makes good on the covered amounts.

This protection is especially important to small companies. In a world plagued by war and political turmoil, dealing with unknown customers in distant nations can be risky business. Loss of a single major contract can spell financial disaster for the exporter.

For this reason, more and more companies are now taking advantage of Eximbank services. Signing up for bank support enables entrepreneurs to tap overseas markets while simultaneously limiting the risk of heavy losses.

Major Eximbank programs for small businesses include:

Comprehensive Bank Guarantees: This plan helps exporters arrange for commercial bank financing. U.S. companies seeking commercial bank funds may apply for Eximbank guarantees on cash payments. Eximbank encourages commercial bank participation by agreeing to reimburse the lender in the event of default by foreign buyers.

Medium-term guarantee plans call for repayment to the banks within a set period ranging from six months to five years. The schedule depends on the type of merchandise involved and on the importer's credit rating.

Foreign Credit Insurance: This short-term plan provides direct protection to U.S. firms engaged in foreign trade. Exporters may purchase insurance policies covering the risks of commercial or political losses overseas. Policies are written by a group of private insurance companies working through Eximbank.

Fees for the insurance and credit-guarantee programs are paid by the exporters. Actual costs are based both on the length of the credit period and the credit standing of the nation of import. Eximbank evaluates the risks involved in dealing with virtually every nation in the world.

Federal officials note that a growing percentage of Eximbank transactions now involve firms with fewer than 10 employees. For this reason, bank executives are becoming more aware of the small exporter's special needs and objectives.

Entrepreneurs may apply for Eximbank services by writing to the Export-Import Bank of the U.S., 8111 Vermont Avenue, N.W., Washington, DC 20531.

PUBLICATIONS

A Basic Guide to Exporting, a general overview of the export field, geared to the potential exporter. Published by the U.S. Government Printing Office

Basics of Export Marketing, a comprehensive list of publications pertaining to the export field. Available from TWA, Director-Freight Sales, P.O. Box 25, Grand Central Station, NY, NY. (free)

California Export Services Guide, a list of more than 1,000 California organizations and businesses that can assist the beginning or expanding exporter increase trade business. Available from the California Department of Commerce, Division of International Trade (free)

Eximbank Programs (Vol 2), a description of the programs offered by the Export-Import Bank of the United States to assist U.S. exporters with selling their goods abroad. Available from the Export-Import Bank (free)

The EMC—Your Export Department, a brief explanation of overseas marketing services provided by Export Management Companies. Available from the U.S. Department of Commerce, Washington, DC. (free)

Export Marketing for Smaller Firms, a step-by-step analysis of how a smaller business can either enter or expand export markets. Published by the Small Business Administration; available from the U.S. Government Printing Office (free)

F.C.I.A. Export Credit Insurance; The Competitive Edge, a marketing brochure detailing the requirements and advantages of FCIA export credit insurance. Available from the Foreign Credit Insurance Association (free)

Foreign Commerce Handbook, a detailed list of government and private organizations, and their export trade-related functions. Available from the U.S. Chamber of Commerce

A Guide to Financing Exports, a brief description of the various agencies that facilitate export financing, with an overview of export financing techniques. Available from the U.S. Department of Commerce, Washington, D.C. (free)

An Introduction to Doing Import and Export Business, a manual outlining procedures for organizing and conducting world trading companies. Available from the U.S. Chamber of Commerce (free)

Management International Business Information Kit, a checklist of business considerations for entering and functioning in the export field. Published by the Southern California Regional Export Expansion Council and available from the U.S. Department of Commerce Field Office in Los Angeles

Marketing Aids for Higher Export Profits, a checklist of the extensive U.S. Department of Commerce publications and export services. Available from the U.S. Department of Commerce, Washington, DC. (free)

World Trade Data Yearbook, Business Abroad Magazine, articles and facts pertaining to world trade. Yearbook comes with the subscription. From Dun & Bradstreet Publications, P.O. Box 2088 Grand Central Station, NY, NY. 10017

DEPARTMENT ADDRESSES

Office of International Trade Promotion,
Bureau of International Commerce,
U.S. Department of Commerce,
Washington, DC. 20230

Superintendent of Documents
U.S. Government Printing Office
Washington, DC. 20402

Foreign Credit Insurance Association
Public Affairs Department
One World Trade Center
N.Y., NY 10048

World Trade Library
One Embarcadero Center
San Francisco, CA 94111

RUNNING IN EVERY DIRECTION:
How to sprint a straight course to business success

We all know the navigator's law that the shortest distance between two points is a straight line. Pit two vessels against one another and the one which follows the law is, in most cases, the one that wins the race.

The same is true in business. While ten would-be business owners may rush from the starter's block at the same instant, only one will get to the top of the heap first—one will reap the rewards of personal wealth while the others are still climbing, foundering or simply scratching for survival. Several will even drop out as failures before the race is over.

What makes the members of the group so different? Why are some winners while others are flat-out losers? And among those who do succeed, why do some get there first? Why are some living on easy street while others are still hoping to make ends meet?

Part of the answer can be found in the way different individuals first face the challenge of business ownership. Those who arrive at the winners' circle first are most often the ones who have borrowed a page from the navigator's notebook: they have remembered to draw that straight line to the top.

In most cases, the losers are marked by a common mistake I call "running in every direction." Like the proverbial chicken with its head cut off, these potential entrepreneurs are so excited with the prospect of business ownership that they lose control right from the start. They are so eager to make millions that they never take the time to draw up a simple game plan. They never really think about all the nuts and bolts functions that must be tackled if a new business is going to experience a successful take-off. The result: they wind up having to redo early mistakes at a later date—wind up going back to the basics when the company should be into its ascent.

What, then, is the solution? How can entrepreneurs race from the starting line first, without having to retrace their steps at a later date? How can business owners learn to draw that straight line to the top?

Well, it is really a lot less complicated than you may think. All you really have to do is take the step-by-step approach to business formation. Make sure you do all the preparatory work from the start, even when the business is still an idea in the back of your mind. (If it is too late for that, have no fear: it is wiser to change your mistakes in midstream than to keep on repeating them.)

What it all boils down to is this: every business is built on a foundation. If the foundation is strong, the business can keep on growing indefinitely without any fear of a cave-in. If the bottom is weak, however, the firm may collapse just as it is poised for its greatest growth. As a result, the path to the top (if it is there at all) becomes crooked and roundabout.

You can avoid this detour (which plagues so many small companies) by learning the seven basic steps to starting a business on a solid foundation. We'll show you how. Why not grab a notebook and jot down the following plans. Think of them as a blueprint for success.

1. The first step is to make sure you are in the right business. You can do this by preparing a "personal aptitude profile" listing your experience, education and personality traits. Be sure these match the requirements of the field you are entering. If this exercise

reveals a serious gap in the skills you need to be successful, try to arrange for a crash course at a local business school or hire an expert trained at this particular function.

If, for example, you are a natural-born inventor—a technical genius—and you are launching a company to sell computer software, your aptitude profile may reveal that you will be weak at one of the major management functions: salesmanship. You can make up for this by either taking a course in personal selling or you may choose to hire a topnotch marketer to do the work. Whatever you decide, you will be starting off on the right foot, with your company well prepared for the challenges ahead.

2. The next consideration is personal finance. If you are leaving an established job to start a venture of your own (as is the case for so many newly-launched entrepreneurs), you must know how much salary you will have to draw from the new business to keep your family afloat until the company takes off. You simply can not run a new business if your personal life is collapsing all around you.

The best way to match your personal financial needs with the new company's initial earnings is to draw up a cost-of-living budget. Compare this with the venture's early revenue projections and make sure you will have enough to get by until the firm really takes hold. If it looks like you will be short, cut back on personal expenses or hold off on starting the business until you can save some money to carry you through.

Use Chart 5 to compute your average cost-of-living.

3. You are now ready to think about the kind of legal organization best suited for your company. There are basically three choices (proprietorship, partnership and corporation) and the wrong selection at the start may wind up costing you substantial sums of money in taxes or personal liabilities. So review the matter carefully. (See Chapter 1 for a full discussion of legal alternatives.)

4. When it comes to business, finances must play a part in any planning process. One of the most important basic plans is the computation of the company's initial cash requirements: exactly how much will be required to get the venture off the ground.

CHART 5

DETAILED BUDGET

Regular Monthly Payments		Personal Expense	
Rent or House Payments (including taxes)	$ ___	Clothing, Cleaning, Laundry, Shoe Repair	$ ___
Car Payments (including insurance)	___	Drugs	___
Appliances/TV Payments	___	Doctors and Dentists	___
Home Improvement Loan Payments	___	Education	___
		Dues	___
Personal Loan Payments	___	Gifts and Contributions	___
Health Plan Payments	___	Travel	___
Life Insurance Premiums	___	Newspapers, Magazines, Books	___
Other Insurance Premiums		Auto Upkeep, Gas and Parking	___
Miscellaneous Payments	___	Spending Money, Allowances	___
TOTAL	$ ═══	TOTAL	$ ═══

Household Operating Expense		Tax Expense	
Telephone	___	Federal and State Income Taxes	$ ___
Gas and Electricity	___	Personal Property Taxes	___
Water	___	Other Taxes	___
Other Household Expenses, Repairs, Maintenance	___	TOTAL	$ ═══
TOTAL	$ ═══	BUDGET SUMMARY	

Food Expense		Regular Monthly Payments	$ ___
		Household Operating Expense	___
Food–At Home	$ ___	Food Expense	$ ═══
Food–Away from Home	___	Personal Expense	
TOTAL	$ ═══	Tax Expense	
		MONTHLY TOTAL	

Knowing this as well as the personal cost-of-living expenses figured earlier will round out the picture on initial financial needs. Use Chart 6 to figure the company's cash needs for the first three months of operation.

Now you have a better idea of the amount of financing you will need up front. The worst mistake of all is underestimating cash requirements and then having to stall or close the business until additional funds can be obtained.

5. Fine tuning your early financial preparations involves drawing up a balance sheet. Put simply, this reflects the company's assets minus its liabilities at any set point in time. The reason for preparing an initial balance sheet is to have a point of reference for the company's progress. Prepare another balance sheet six months and then one year later in order to monitor the firm's progress (or lack of it).

A typical balance sheet is shown in Chart 7.

6. Since no business exists in a vacuum, you will want to do some research into the kinds of competition your company will be facing. Just how much competition there is—and how it is set up—will have a pervasive influence on the way your firm will perform. Knowing exactly what you are facing from the start will help you to prepare for competitive hurdles. Competition will, for example, influence your choice of location, prices, merchandise lines, and promotional strategies. Find out what you are facing before you get involved in any of these activities. (See Chapter 3 for tips on using free U.S. Census Bureau data for determining the extent of local competition.)

7. Last, but certainly not least, is this simple precaution. Don't make a move until you survey all the rules, laws and regulations applicable to your business. You will want to be sure to be completely within the law before selling a single product. Make sure to touch bases with the following authorities, at the very minimum:

> state and local tax administrations
> a local office of the Internal Revenue Service
> state and local consumer affairs offices
> state and local licensing agencies

CHART 6
THREE-MONTH CHART
(Fill in Expense Only if Required)

	From last paycheck to opening day	$ _____
LIVING EXPENSES	Moving expense	_____
	For three months after opening day (from cost-of-living budget)	_____
	Salaries	_____
	Last month's business rent (1st three months in operating expenses below)	_____
DEPOSITS,	Telephone and utility deposits	_____
PREPAYMENTS,	Sales tax deposit	_____
LICENSES	Business licenses	_____
	Insurance premiums	_____
	Remodeling and redecorating	_____
LEASEHOLD	Fixtures, equipment, displays	_____
IMPROVEMENTS	Installation labor	_____
	Signs—outside and inside	_____
INVENTORY	Service, delivery equipment, and supplies	_____
	Merchandise (approximately 65% of this amount to be invested in opening stock)	_____

TOTAL OPERATING EXPENSES FOR THREE MONTHS   _____

RESERVE TO CARRY CUSTOMERS' ACCOUNTS   _____

CASH FOR PETTY CASH, CHANGE, ETC.   _____

                                          TOTAL $ _____

CHART 7
BALANCE SHEET

CURRENT ASSETS	
Cash	
Accounts Receivable	
Inventory	
FIXED ASSETS	
Real Estate	
Fixtures and Equipment	
Vehicles	
OTHER ASSETS	
License	
Goodwill	
TOTAL ASSETS	
CURRENT LIABILITIES	
Notes Payable (due within 1 year)	
Accounts Payable	
Accrued Expenses	
Taxes Owed	
LONG-TERM LIABILITIES	
Notes Payable (due after 1 year)	
Other	
TOTAL LIABILITIES	
NET WORTH (Assets minus Liabilities)	
TOTAL LIABILITIES plus NET WORTH	

local offices of the Occupational Safety and
Health Administration, the Consumer Product Safety Commission, the Social Security
Administration and the Labor Department
local zoning commissions

Since it is often difficult for business owners to keep up-to-date on all legal requirements, I recommend a comprehensive consultation with an experienced lawyer, accountant, banker and insurance agent.

These talks will likely add more steps to your checklist. Be patient and do them all. Remember, you are building a foundation for future growth. You want to sprint that straight line to the top.

PAYING THROUGH THE NOSE:
How to learn secrets of money-saving business services

Sometimes companies are guilty of committing common mistakes not by what they do—but by what they fail to do. They are, in effect, guilty by omission.

To see what we mean by this, let's take a close look at a very real example. In recent years, businesses of all kinds—large and small—have been buffeted by extremely steep cost increases in operating expenses. Across-the-board inflation in everything from labor to raw materials to utilities have pulled a one-two punch on many a profit statement.

In a typical reaction, however, the smarter and better-run outfits have found new ways to keep down the spiraling cost of doing business. Rather than continuing to pay through the nose, they have hit on little cost-cutting secrets that can save many thousands of dollars a year.

Business owners who sit silently watching their costs go through the roof are prime examples of those entrepreneurs guilty by omission. You, however, can avoid this mistake. You can take advantage of the following cost-cutting secrets we have picked up from savvy entrepreneurs and are now passing on to you.

Auctions: Surveys of retail store activities indicate that sales and bargains are still the prime catalysts for consumer spending. After years of trading up to higher-priced lines, consumers are once again seeking maximum value.

The surveys conducted by independent consulting firms note that the dual demons of inflation and recession have forced consumers to pay renewed attention to price appeal. More and more shoppers are resisting higher prices—holding out for special sales and patronizing discount shops.

Aggressive merchants are capitalizing on this trend by prolonging seasonal sales, reducing traditional profit margins and offering lower-priced lines for budget-conscious customers. A good many small merchants, in fact, are radically changing merchandising tactics, transforming full-service stores to clearance centers. This positions the stores as cutrate outlets specializing in the kinds of bargains consumers are seeking.

Smaller, more flexible firms find it easy to adapt to this changing market. Owner-managers are generally in touch with customer demands and are rarely tied to specific manufacturers or product lines. Changing the merchandise mix is simply a matter of finding alternate suppliers.

Rather than dealing with low-priced distributors, however, many merchants are buying at auction. Auctions enable merchants to benefit in two ways: they can buy top-quality goods at rock-bottom prices and can earn a reputation for exceptional discounts. The approach is just right for today's value minded consumers.

A retail survey reports that a shoe merchant typical of many small businessmen turned to auction purchases to cope with escalating product prices. The merchant reported that profits of more than 100 percent are quite common for merchandise purchased at auction. Brand-name shoes originally selling for $25 can, for example, be purchased at auction for $5 a pair. Although the bidder must buy large quantities—perhaps 500 pairs—the potential profit makes the investment worthwhile. Figuring an average selling price of $15 per pair, total profit may approach $5,000. In addition, the merchant attracts a loyal following of regular customers.

Getting in on exceptional purchases is not as difficult as it may appear. Businessmen may bid at any number of auctions featuring a wide variety of consumer goods. Auction calendars are listed in local business journals, industry publications and trade association newsletters. Interested parties are generally free to attend without cost or obligation.

Auction activities are, in fact, on the rise. Poor economic conditions have pushed up the bankruptcy rate, forcing a great number of firms to liquidate assets at the auction block. Alert merchants can capitalize on these sales by purchasing an entire inventory of up-to-date merchandise below original cost.

Special purchase merchandise may be used as loss leaders to build store traffic or may be used to complement higher-priced lines. Merchants considering a discount-only operation, however, must first be assured of a steady supply of low-priced goods. This means working with manufacturers, auctioneers and large chain stores to get the first rights to liquidations, excess production and discontinued lines.

Whether or not discounting is right for your firm, it's always a good idea to keep your options open. Merchants should seek and maintain contacts in the auction, special purchase markets.

Business Liquidation Auctions: Learning to bid and deal at business liquidation auctions helps entrepreneurs save money on equipment purchases. Prices at liquidation sales tend to be 20 to 30 per cent lower than prevailing retail rates.

Finding a liquidation sale is simple enough. The increasing number of liquidations across the nation are prompting auctions for every type of business equipment from heavy machinery to office furniture. Unable to cope with the strains of a sagging economy, more and more firms are closing up and selling out. Valuable assets are going to the highest bidder, often at bargain prices.

Once dominated by dealers and corporate agents, liquidations auctions are now heavily attended by entrepreneurs representing their own firms. Eighty percent of the purchases at liquidation sales, in fact, are made by the users themselves. The absence of the middleman reduces prices even further.

Lower purchase prices enable management to arrange

internal financing rather than seeking bank credit. This cuts red tape, assures the availability of funds and eliminates the need to pay current high interest rates. The net result, reduced overhead, is especially important in a period of slow or declining sales.

Saving money, however, is not the only reason small businessmen are flocking to liquidation auctions. Speed of delivery is another important benefit. At a time when factory orders for specialized industrial equipment are backed up two or three years, managers need an alternate source of supply to meet pressing needs. Auctions provide the perfect solution. Purchased equipment can often be bought, shipped, delivered and placed in operation in a matter of days.

Managers may keep up with liquidation auction activities by checking newspaper ads, trade magazine calendars and direct mail promotions. Announcements indicate the type of equipment to be auctioned, as well as the dates, locations and general terms. Liquidation sales may be for a specific type of equipment or may include a bankrupt firm's total assets such as vehicles, adding machines, conveyers and office desks. Managers may opt to bid on one or all of the featured items.

Experienced buyers visit auction sites in advance of the sale in order to carefully analyze each piece of equipment. Once the bidding starts, there is little time for close inspection. The auctioneer and his audience move from item to item, selling one after another in rapid succession. Since all goods are sold "as is," buyers are responsible for removing equipment from the auction site.

Typical industrial auctions sell from $50,000 to millions of dollars worth of equipment, last from one day to two-weeks, take place in a plant or a store, and are attended by from 40 to 500 buyers. Sales may be sponsored by the owners or by auction specialists.

Bartering: The age-old practice of bartering is back again—gaining renewed popularity as a secondary market for products and services. For small businesses, the timing could not be better.

Faced with tougher-than-ever competition for the buying dollar, many firms often find themselves stacked to the rafters with excess merchandise. Over-production, extravagant purchasing and consumer resistance combine to bloat inventories beyond the danger zone. At this point, management usually cleans house at clearance prices and swallows the losses without a fight.

Modern bartering (also known as reciprocal trade) offers a more profitable solution. Put simply, bartering lets you trade what you have too much of for what you need or want. The service is boon to small companies threatened by an avalanche of deadwood inventory.

Here's how it works. Let's say a retailer accepts delivery of a hot new product management believes will sell like there's no tomorrow. Based on this optimistic projection, the firm doubles its usual order for new items and sets out to promote it heavily. Within three weeks the results are clear: the product proves to be a total flop. Sales are minimal at best and the merchant is stuck with a large and costly inventory. At this point, management can either hold a clearance sale or can turn instead to professional barterers.

In many cases, bartering is the wiser choice. That is because barterers credit you for the full wholesale value of all unwanted merchandise. There is no need to sacrifice quality goods at cut-rate prices. In addition, barterers will take the entire inventory off your hands almost immediately—that's a feat few clearance sales can accomplish.

Instead of cash payments, however, many barterers offer you a wide variety of goods and services including advertising time or space, new automobiles, trucks, hotel and restaurant credits and even business insurance. The list goes on and on and changes according to the bartering firm you deal with. Many will even go out of their way to get something special for you if that is what it will take to make a trade possible.

Barterers exchange their products and services for your excess inventory. You select any one or a combination of items equal to the wholesale value of the merchandise you are giving up. Barterers remove the goods from your store or warehouse and may even pay for insurance and storage should the movement be delayed.

Bartering can also be used to acquire business products and services at less than usual costs—up to 50 per cent less. To see how this works, let's take the real case of a small firm manufacturing a new line of inexpensive telephone devices. To get the product off the ground, a good deal of expensive sales travel was necessary.

Management cut costs in this area by bartering its own excess telephone devices for hotel room credits. The firm traded 5,000 devices with a wholesale value of $5 each for credits worth $25,000 retail at a national hotel chain. Since the devices cost the manufacturer only $12,500 to produce, it actually purchased the hotel credits at half the going rate. A bartering firm handled all the details, exchanging the excess devices for hotel credits acquired in a previous deal.

Managers interested in exploring this concept may ask trade groups or business associates for the name of a local barterer. Or you may call Atwood Richards, Inc., a large bartering outfit with offices across the nation. The number is 212-490-9200. Operators will put you in touch with the local office nearest to you.

Interconnect Services: Ma Bell, that kindly old symbol of the telephone industry, is worried these days. Ever since the Federal Communications Commission issued its 1968 landmark decision enabling businesses to buy equipment from outside sources rather than renting from Bell, the phone company has lost hundreds of thousands of customers to this new competition. What really worries Ma Bell is that this trend is now accelerating.

"It's clear to us that more and more private businesses are indeed turning away from the major companies and are turning instead to other sources for telephone equipment," says an FCC attorney. "These users insist they get a better deal from alternate suppliers than from Bell, better in terms of price and equipment."

The major difference between Bell and its competitors is basic: Bell rents equipment; the others sell it. Buying directly from the so-called "interconnect" outfits puts an end to monthly rental charges, an attractive benefit for small companies. Purchased equipment is simply hooked up to Bell's lines and is serviced by the interconnect suppliers.

"The cost of the interface is so small," says Leonard

London, president of Telecommunications Systems, Inc. of Greenwich, Conn., "that it is really insignificant when compared to the overall savings we deliver. Bell has tried to use this to make our service less attractive, but it hasn't worked."

"The reason for our success is simple: we can save business a good deal of money," adds a Telecommunications Systems sales representative.

"Take the case of a hypothetical company with a key telephone system using 20 phones and 12 trunk lines. We could save that firm about $235 per month for equipment for the first five years of use. Then, after the payout period, the savings would be about $600 per month. What's more, management gets an immediate 10 percent tax credit in the year of purchase."

"We have the most sophisticated equipment available anywhere. For example, we have automatic privacy as standard equipment on intercoms and trunk calls. That means no one can interrupt sensitive business calls. We also have hands free intercoms which enable the busy executive to speak with his secretary without breaking off continuing calls. And the important thing is we supply many of these capabilities for less costs than Bell charges for standard equipment."

Bell's response is twofold. While the company insists its equipment is on par with all other suppliers, a spokesman admits Bell's prices are often higher. "We are in an unenviable position," says Bell spokesman Marilyn Laurie. "We have to charge higher rates to business in order to recoup losses we often sustain in providing essential residential services. Interconnect firms, on the other hand, can focus solely on the most lucrative markets."

The big winners are the nation's businesses. Competition has led to a steady stream of new equipment and services. Small companies with even limited telephone systems (six or more phones) should explore the alternatives. The savings may be considerable.

These are just a few examples of how a willingness to explore the unconventional can save your company more money—and can put more cash in a personal account. Take a close look at all of your high-cost services and see if you can't find "a better way" for each.

GIVING IN TO BANKRUPTCY:
How to win your company a second chance

Okay, so it happens! What you feared most all along—the bankruptcy of your company—actually happens. What do you do?

Although you never really thought or talked about it much (probably because of the fear of doing so), the possibility of bankruptcy was always in the back of your mind. You knew that it happens to thousands of companies every year and that yours could be one of them. You knew that you could put all of your money, talent and sweat into a business of your own—live with it and nurture it for years—and then only have it go sour on you in the end. Leaving you with nothing—holding an empty bag.

Unfortunately, this happens all the time. And, in a good many cases, there is really no one to blame. Life is not always so clear cut that we can point an accusing finger and identify the guilty. The same is true in business. The owner-manager may do just about everything right and still find that the business has gone down the tubes. The trouble may result from a variety of factors including casualty losses, dire economic conditions and competitive pressures.

So what hope is there for the capable manager who knows

183

how to run a successful business yet finds his company in serious trouble? Does he simply give up the dream of self-employment? Does he throw in the towel and chalk it all up to the fates? Or can he stand in place, fight it out and win a second chance for his company?

The answer is clear: if you want a second chance badly enough, you can probably fight for and win it. The problem is, most entrepreneurs make the mistake of thinking they must give up and run at the first sign of insolvency. They make the tragic mistake of failing to fight for what they worked so hard to build.

The truth is this: bankruptcy is not necessarily the end. Even the most depleted firms can reorganize and win a fresh lease on a prosperous new life.

"You talk about being dedicated to a business and you are talking about me," says Irving I. of Saddlebrook, NJ. "I built Split Age Technology, my custom machinery company, from the ground up. My dream since childhood was to have a company of my own, so I left a good-paying aerospace job, plunked down $32,000 of life savings and worked 20 hours a day for four years to make a go of it.

"And I was successful. I kept up with technological developments and earned an MBA in night school. The hard work and expertise paid off: sales zoomed from zero to $3.7 million per year and I was confident that Split Age Technology was on the way to the big time."

Then, quite unexpectedly, business tragedy struck. All at once, several of Irv's largest machine orders were returned to him as defective. Customers were grumbling, bad news was spreading and refunds had to be paid. The source of the trouble turned out to be a component part made by an ordinarily-reliable supplier—something beyond Irv's control.

Although Irv tried to delay the rush for refunds, his efforts were of little avail. Everyone wanted new machines or complete reimbursement immediately, and this tremendous pressure was simply too much for the firm to handle. It wasn't long before creditors had the firm in bankruptcy proceedings.

"Although I was far from happy with this development," Irv

says, "to me it was only round one. There was no way I was going to walk away from a company I had built from scratch—no way I would walk away from a life's dream. And you know something, I didn't have to.

"I hired an experienced attorney, worked with my creditors and managed to put the company back on the map. I made good to all customers, rebuilt my reputation and learned to set up a system of quality controls for component parts. Today, my company is one of the largest of its kind in the east: we just passed the $20 million annual sales mark. I have 230 employees, healthy profits and a determination to go right to the top. This time I'll make it."

Unlike Humpty Dumpty who fell from the wall, a bankrupt business can be put together again. And it doesn't take "all the kings horses and all the kings men" to pull it off. A competent attorney experienced in bankruptcy laws will do. That is because federal regulations are designed to breathe new life into vanquished firms. In many cases, there is a second chance to right the wrongs—to turn things around and try again.

What are the options? What happens when the cash register is empty and creditors are waiting in line? What happens when a business is legally bankrupt?

"Management does have a number of options," says Robert Webber, staff attorney for the Small Business Administration (SBA). "The precise course of action, however, depends on management's commitment to the company and on the attitude of the creditors.

"In most cases, for bankruptcy to proceed, the company must be insolvent. That is, liabilities must exceed assets and the firm must be proven unable to meet its financial obligations. Once this is established, further action may be taken."

The following are the major forms of bankruptcy actions:

Straight Bankruptcy: This may be a voluntary or an involuntary action, prompted by the debtor or the creditors. In involuntary actions, creditors file a bankruptcy claim against a debtor company, alleging that the firm is insolvent. The action is filed with a bankruptcy judge—part of the federal district court system.

Owner-managers subject to this action must reveal all relevant business records to the court. Here, management may contest the action of the creditors claiming that the company is not insolvent and is capable of meeting its obligations. If the decision is for the creditors, managers may still appeal to the district court.

"Small business owners seeking to save their firms should come to these proceedings well prepared," says Webber. "If they lose the action, the court will appoint a trustee to seize the company's assets and sell them off for cash. The creditors will then be paid."

Reorganization: Better known as "chapter ten," reorganization offers the insolvent business the opportunity to get back on a sound financial footing. The procedure, which is voluntary, gives the company a reasonable period of time to get its affairs in order and to establish a plan for the repayment of creditors.

In this type of action, a court-appointed trustee operates the business during the reorganization period. The trustee prepares a payment schedule and reports this to the court for approval. If all goes well the firm may resume operations under new guidelines and may try once again for commercial success.

Chapter Eleven: Basically a contractual agreement between the creditors and the debtor, "chapter eleven" proceedings use the machinery of the bankruptcy court to bring both sides together on common ground.

Actually another form of reorganization, chapter eleven enables the parties to the action to agree on a negotiated settlement.

The objective here is to give the company a second chance—to save the firm for the benefit of all concerned. Management hopes to revive the failing venture; creditors hope for full payment.

"Whatever option the owner-manager takes, involvement in a bankruptcy does not eliminate all chances for future business dealings," Webber adds. "Although it is a mark against the individual's credit rating, the old stigma concerning bankruptcy is fading. Our society takes a much more liberal view of this now."

So remember that in business you can get a second chance. Be prepared to fight for it. You deserve it.

"Being involved in bankruptcy proceedings was not the end of the line I thought it would be," adds Art L. of Port Arthur, Texas. "When an uninsured casualty loss put my fuel oil distributorship in the red, and the creditors were on my back, I used chapter eleven to keep hold of the business.

"What I did can serve as a guide for many businesses caught in the same circumstances:

> *Bend over backwards to accommodate your creditors
> *Agree to a regular repayment scale that will both satisfy the creditors and yet keep your firm afloat
> *Honor all payment commitments as they are made
> *Keep creditors fully up-to-date on the company's recovery
> *Try to identify the original problem and take firm steps to prevent its recurrence"

Art came out of chapter eleven clean as a whistle, still running a solid distributorship ready to resume its agressive growth. His prompt repayment of all debts not only pleased creditors but also impressed existing and potential customers.

"When it was all over, my company was stronger than ever before. That's the best reason I can give for sticking it out."

We agree.

INDEX

* <u>Speak to Gentile</u> —

* <u>Speak to Marketing expert</u>
how to Market to Spiritual crowd.
Market that appreciates items
w/ a soul. Minimal but
exotic⊙
How do i market that?

* <u>SCORE REPRESENTATIVE</u>

* <u>BANKER</u> ⌐ LOCAL ⌐

⌐ BIZ OWNERS ⌐
* ANKI
* CHRISTINA
* GREGG
*

GOALS FOR ~~THIS MONTH~~.

- GO TO MEDITATION CLASS ⊚
- CALL INNER LIGHT CENTER ⊙
- ▓▓ NEW SCHOOL ⟦ * TODAY * ⟧
- PAUL WILLING TO
    TEACH ME ELECTRIC
        GUITAR?

- WILL MOM'S INSURANCE
    PAY FOR BABY?

- **FIND A JOB** THAT
  STILL PAYS #1000. A
        MONTH FOR INVESTMENTS
    PLUS SOME. FOR P/T
        WK.

-

BABY STEPS, BABY STEPS, BABY STEPS
    AND SMILE
        IN
        THE PRESENT.

ONE

<u>~~XXXXX~~ FINE NIGHT</u>

CB 12:09 P.M 63°C

AND I'M FEELING FINE
CROSSING THE
BROOKLYN BRIDGE

BIRDS DO NOT
REST ON AN UNSOUND
STRUCTURE
THERE ARE NO BIRDS
ON THE BROOKLYN BRIDGE

THIS IS A PRETTY COOL
CITY AFTER ALL
" I'M GOING BACK TO
NYC I THINK IVE
HAD ENOUGH "